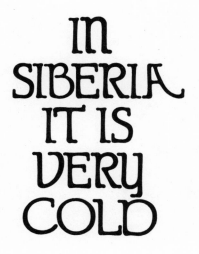

IN SIBERIA IT IS VERY COLD

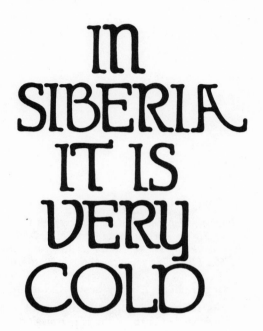

IN SIBERIA IT IS VERY COLD

Lester Goldberg

DEMBNER BOOKS • NEW YORK

DEMBNER BOOKS
Published by Red Dembner Enterprises Corp.,
80 Eighth Avenue, New York, N.Y. 10011
Distributed by W. W. Norton & Company, Inc.,
500 Fifth Avenue, New York, N.Y. 10110

Portions of this book originally appeared in *Ascent* (Vol. 4, No. 2-1979); *Cimarron Review* (Oct. 1980, No. 53, and Oct. 1982, No. 61); and *Here's the Story: Fiction with Heart* (The Spirit That Moves Us Press, 1985).

Library of Congress Cataloging in Publications Data

Goldberg, Lester, 1924 –
    In Siberia it is very cold.

    I. Title.
PS3557.035781S 1987   813'.54   86-29172
ISBN 0-934878-88-9

To Dorothy

PREFACE

In the fall of 1939 the German Army swiftly overran Poland. Refugees, Jewish and Gentile, fled toward the Russian border. The Russians, suspicious of anyone arriving from the West, interned the refugees and sent many of them to Siberia to work in logging camps. Shortly after the Germans invaded Russia in June 1941, the Polish government, in exile in London, signed an agreement with the Soviet Union that freed all Polish nationals. Polish citizens in the Siberian labor camps were given the chance to relocate to cities in Asiatic Russia: Chymkent, Tashkent, or Alma Ata, two thousand miles southeast of Moscow and fifty miles from the Chinese border.

A number of Poles from Zamoscz chose Alma Ata, called Father of Apples, because they heard it was a warm place where food was plentiful.

ONE

If we choose a Jew to give out the bread and dole out the cup of water for each person, he could never resist the women asking for more for their children. So I join with the others: we pass by Kaplan, the silent teacher, and Velvel, the actor, and choose Kafchinski, the eldest and a Polish gentile, as leader of the cattle car. Kafchinski gives one loaf to each four and cuts a quarter loaf for one day's ration for each single man. Those who get the rounded end

complain. The Pole just waves them off and con-
tinues cutting the black loaves.

I count forty souls. The families stake out their
space by placing bundles around them in a square. It
stinks here, in the bachelor's corner, next to the head-
high partition. Inside is the single hole in the floor
that all use. I get up to count again. Only thirty-eight
souls now. I've made it my job to count them every
day, but I never get the same number. I step over
shoes tied with cord, cavalry boots, feet wrapped in
rags, and walk to the other end of the car to peer
through the cut-out car side. I chew my dry bread
and wash it down with warm water.

The grassy steppe flows by day after day: long
sunburnt vistas to the right; to the left, broken by a
river, moving dots at a distance, maybe horses,
maybe oxen, a single wooden hut, then a few round
huts of the nomads—days of this, for a thousand
kilometers—no change. Silver birches along the
waterways and sometimes a solid black wood, then
the plains again.

An unexpected cabbage soup appears that night.
"Are we in Siberia yet?" I ask the Russian trainman
who drops a sack of bread at the Pole's feet. He
shakes his head. "Nyet."

Wrapped in my blanket, and next to that great
lump, Berchik, I dream about father, mother, and my
sisters, all sitting down to a Friday night feast.
Mother heaps stuffed cabbage on my plate and then a
heavy hand smacks me across the forehead. Berchik
thrashes about on his back, moaning, flailing out with
both fists. I shake his shoulder. He grows rigid. "Can
the Germans come this far, Max?"

"No. We're thousands of miles away. Stop worrying."

When I turned fourteen and was apprenticed to a barber, Berchik, only two years older, came to work for my father. Even then, he could wrap his great arms around a herring barrel and boost it into the wagon unaided. When Berchik's team waited in line, the toughest Polish drayman didn't dare push his way in front to load. With a few blows of his fists, he could smash a man to the ground. He fought for a few zlotys, for a chicken, a bottle of schnapps. He beat the heavy-footed ones, but I remember a clever boxer cutting him up badly in Lublin. And when he hadn't moved out of the way quick enough to suit three German soldiers, they beat him insensible with rifle butts and boots. Lucky they didn't know blond Berchik was a Jew. Just a fresh Pole, they thought, so they didn't finish him off.

Berchik rolls toward the car side, pulls his jacket over his head.

I can't sleep and sit up next to my snoring friend, clasp my legs, hug them to me. I used to feel safe in Berchik's shadow. I reach in my pocket for a dry crust and chew until it softens, hold it on my tongue, until it tastes like bread.

Gray dawn steals into the car. Sleeping forms all around. A hacking cough. Two together, moving as one, under a blanket. The groom's skullcap bobs on his head. His bride's brown wig lies to one side. I can see the crown of her kerchief-covered head. The tremors travel along the car floor to me, under me. I look at the wall. Let them finish thumping in private. Someone sits up at my other side and I sense the outline of Velvel's round belly. I pat it and turn to him. "Smile for me, Velvel. I'll give you a haircut later. Free!"

He licks his soft, tiny lips. Looks into my mouth, watching me chew. A Viennese actor, the first day he entertained us with impersonations, pieces from *Othello*. Now he wolfs his bread and sits all day guarding the fancy leather suitcase.

I stand up to escape the dumb hunger in his eyes, stumble over the bridegroom, and give him a little kick in the ribs on my way to the window. In a short while, he gets up, the lucky devil; he begins winding the black phylacteries around one arm and while he winds, does a little practice swaying. The same unbroken steppes. Dry and yellow and I savor the warm June air.

When the Germans overran Zamoscz, I went to the barber shop as usual. We heard from the West, but where could we run? My father loaded his wagon at the railroad, in German hands like everything else. We worked for them. Maybe they're not so bad, one teamster said. But Jews started to disappear. Jambro's wife washed clothes for them and they drowned her eight-year-old child, in front of her, in her own washtub. When I heard this, then met her in the street, tearing out clumps of hair, I ran home. House empty. Clothes scattered on the floor. I pried up the floorboard under father's bed, found only a handful of zlotys, stuffed them in my pocket. Ran next door. Worse here, kitchen table overturned, dishes broken, curtains torn down, flower pots and geraniums lying smashed on the curtains. I fled and went around to the back, jumped the rear fence, skirted the community bathhouse and ran through the back alleys, dodging dogs, climbing fences until I came to a little-used dirt road that I followed to the outskirts of town, then threw myself behind a hedge when I heard the engines of the motorcycle patrol.

I have the urge so I go behind the partition. Relieve myself and splatter the rails below. Then I draw my comb and scissors from my bundle. I approach Velvel who sits cross-legged, staring at his belly. Pulling him to his feet, I steer him to an upturned wooden box. He sits. I comb and cut. How good it feels to do my work. "Next." Velvel rises, smiles the helpless little smile and the car lights up.

Kaplan, the French professor, honors me. A reader, he never speaks to me. I trim his gray hair, shaping it in the back. Snick-snick cutting the air with my scissors and on to his tiny beard. I brush his suit jacket off. He starts to rise. I hold him back, hand on one bony shoulder. I call for a mirror. Many are watching us. We are entertainers. The bride shyly hands me a round hand mirror with a gold back. My mother had one. I raise it back of Kaplan's head. I pick up my shaving mirror and hold it before his eyes. "How do you like it?" I say in Yiddish. Then in Polish. He merely nods and rises to his feet like a giraffe I saw on my only trip to Warsaw.

The train pulls into a bare wooden platform. It doesn't move for hours. I look out. No one stirring. A hand truck stands near the station shack. A red geranium hides in a window. Two horses browse behind a fence. My father, if he were here, would trade for the horses in a minute.

We lie at the station all day. No one explains. And

the next day, we eat cold cabbage soup. I notch the car wall with my knife. Five lines, a cross for the days with soup. Eight lines, three crosses. Soup every two or three days. Thirteen lines—fourteen lines, five crosses. Four circles for the couplings of the bride and groom.

At last, we stop at a station cut out from the tall, evergreen forest. My father's watch reads three P.M. Two cars empty out, perhaps eighty souls, no young children. Two Russians are waiting for us, pistols in holsters at their sides. Our Pole, Kafchinski, tells us to load our belongings into the wagons. The wagons pulled by two horses are driven off, in single file, down a narrow track through the forest. Kafchinski gives us a second water ration drawn from a wooden vat next to the station. We drink and then the older Russian starts down the road and we follow his boots. I look back and see the other guard patting his holster and tapping his foot as we file by. We walk all night. I pull Velvel along. Force him to get up. I hold his arm until he catches the rhythm. The skeleton, Kaplan, walks well. Berchik's broad back is always ahead of me; he helps a woman along, then a man. As dawn filters through the green, he's supporting a man whose feet move but with no will of their own.

We enter a clearing in the woods. Soup in big kettles waits on log tables. I hear the train was three days late. The soup has been waiting three days. I eat my share, find half a potato in it, and with a crust of bread saved in my pocket, I wipe the bowl clean.

A new Russian arrives. Without a gun, and sweating in a short coat. Sweat steams his eyeglasses. He reads names and turns pages, licking his two fingers with his tongue—more names—turns the page with his wet finger—licks again—calls my name, Berchik, Velvel and Kaplan together, followed by Kafchinski, his wife Sofia, and their two half-grown children. Other names, another lick, another page. I suspect he is Jewish from this trademan's habit I have seen in yard goods stores, other shops. All the storekeepers licked this way when turning ledgers to mark down credit.

Finally, he gives his name, Dmitri. Not Lazar or Mosher but Dmitri. Now I'm sure. Only a Jew would assume such a common Russian name as a disguise. We follow him down the only street, wooden log buildings on either side, no one about, not a dog, not a child, and on to the farthest end to our quarters. Each building has three doors, side by side. If the buildings were not there, it would look like a vast parade ground surrounded by forest. The entrance runs from front to back, two doors off each side. One room for each family. Each group shares a stone stove, a metal plate across the top. So we have privacy, unless you look underneath the partition, which comes down from the ceiling and stops one foot above the stove. I look under and meet Kafchinski's stony stare.

In the dining room, the following morning, we wash down our bread with strong tea. One hundred men and a few women, in rough clothing. The newcomers stand out by their stylish garments. At the next table, the bride huddles near her husband, the brown wig a little lopsided on her head. The husband still with that black yarmulke on his head as if it could protect him against lightning, a falling tree, anything. Sofia comes from the kitchen, carrying a metal pitcher with more tea. The old timers ignore us, except for one with the gnarled hands of a shoemaker. He leans across the table, black eyes surrounded by beard and says, "To work is to die."

We follow Dmitri into the woods, along a path that suddenly appears at the edge of the square. I stick close to Berchik. He carries a two-handed saw. Dmitri has a folded newspaper sticking out of one pocket. I carry two axes. We pass an area of cut-down trees. Stump after stump. The sun lights the clearing. Velvel also carries a two-handed saw. Dmitri must have been fooled by Velvel's magnificent stomach and imposing height. He pairs me with Berchik. "Meet your quota," he says handing me six metal wedges. "Clean the trunk after the tree is felled. Drop the tree away from the road." When will he speak Yiddish, this Dmitri? Berchik stands like a stone giant.

"What's the quota?" I ask.

"You'll find out," Dmitri says. "Stack the side branches of the same size together. If you drop a tree across the road, you'll work all night to clear it."

Before the others are out of sight, Berchik and I, on either end of the saw, begin cutting. Cut and rest. Wedge so the blade doesn't bind. Cut, cut, sweat, a larger wedge. The tree crashes, hits a stump, shudders and rolls off. We trim with the axes. Stack. Another tree. Build a small fire for tea. Eat bread and drink tea. Trim the third tree, and while we are trimming and it grows darker, we see men dragging back along the road. We stop and join them.

In our room, I find Velvel stretched out on the straw. The teacher sits on the floor, head hanging

down. He doesn't look up. I touch Velvel with my
foot. He groans. "Up, Velvel, time to eat." One hand
over his face, he waves me away. I tug at his arm.
Dead weight. Berchik hauls him to his feet. With me
holding one of his arms and Berchik the other, we
march Velvel off to the dining hall. Kaplan follows.

Cabbage soup and bread. Black-eyes stops in back
of me, leans over, "Fools, you did too much. Your
names will go up on the board. Two big trees, that's
all. Three small ones, trimmed."

The next night, Berchik and I are given extra sugar,
a piece of dried beef. We slow down. Just soup. We
learn to start a tree, leave it standing and use it for
next day's quota. Hunger forces us, after a week, to
cut more. Again, we are rewarded. Velvel and Kaplan
look at us with hatred, but they don't dare say
anything. We need more rest. Always hungry. One
week becomes another. No more rewards. Driven by
hunger, we try to cut more. They've raised the quota.
No more meat.

I get up early and sneak out of our room. The old
timers have been assigned garden plots. I go to one.
Where potatoes have been dug out, I kneel down and
dig a few more from the ground. I brush away my
footprints. Smooth down the prints as I back out until
I reach the grass. I hope these few won't be missed. If
I cook them at home? No. Velvel is slowly selling all
he owns from his big brown suitcase for food. Soon,
he'll have an empty suitcase and the clothes on his
back. He eats at all times, without us.

I save the potatoes, bake them in our tea fire, and
share with Berchik at our lunch break. Now I steal
every week. Always a different garden plot. I branch

out, steal carrots and turnips. A little here, a little there. My mother used to say, look at our prince, he won't eat turnips. If I'm caught? The air grows colder in September. In October, the first snowfall, hard stinging pellets that drive into any crack in your clothing and burn the skin.

Kaplan, the teacher, grows thinner. He never speaks and throws himself down on the straw after our soup and lies there until morning. The actor's legs are beginning to swell.

One night, I hear groans. I listen for the night sounds of old Kafchinski and his hefty Sophia next door. A shadow rises before me. The door opens and closes. To my left, Berchink snores. Kaplan is quiet, yet I think he never sleeps. I go to the door and see Velvel walking in the snow, his arms outstretched like a sleepwalker. I throw on my coat and follow. I grab his arm.

"I can't see anything," he says. "Not the footlights or the woods, the snow—nothing."

I turn him around, lead him back, speak gently, "It's night blindness, Velvel. From the poor food. Believe me, that's all it is. You'll be all right in the morning."

Great luck! A snowstorm the following day, and we can't be sent out to work. After breakfast, I get permission to give haircuts in the dining hall. I work and collect potatoes, carrots, a scissors, two cups, other stuff. Even the three policemen with guns come for a haircut. Three policemen control three hundred and fifty people. Once, they said, someone ran off— walked to the railhead, intending to smuggle himself aboard. The train never arrived. He froze to death. The forests, the steppes imprison us. The commandant (and I admit he lives in one room like the rest of us), gives me a half day off to cut hair once a week.

On this day, when my customers leave for the forest, I linger in the dining hall, pretending to clean my comb. When Sofia comes in to wipe the table, the devil possesses me and I say to her, "I dream of you, in bed at night." Her old one, Kafchinski, cuts wood every day but I never hear the sounds of love from their room.

She brings me a big bowl of cereal laced with honey and then tells me to follow her into the woods. So many petticoats on her, and two dresses—she rests back in a crotch of a low tree, pulls back all the folds, and with my pants around my ankles, I bang her. Then on two October Wednesdays, oatmeal and honey and in the storeroom, standing up. She smelled of turpentine. Maybe she used it to delouse herself. I was clean until I started up with her, then I began to itch—until I thought I'd go crazy. She is so old, almost forty, with mammoth breasts that I hold on to. Not at all like the soft, round girl of the train who has cast aside her wig, and whose cake is rising, rising, as her red-bearded husband grows more gaunt each day.

November, it is back in the woods again—bitter cold. Sofia's hair falls down, her comb drops from her bun and I scrabble on the ground to find it while she urges me, "Faster, faster—we must get back." Then she tires of me, thank God, but the oatmeal still appears on Wednesday.

One night of an oatmeal day, Velvel shakes his

empty suitcase at me. "The pot is empty," he says, "all the trade goods are gone."

"Smile for us, Velvel. Light up the room." I pull some carrots from my pocket. "Here, good for night blindness."

He takes them and chews with little clipping bites. "I need more than rabbit food to smile."

From another pocket, I hand him a fire-blackened potato. I can be generous on my oatmeal day.

He hoists himself to his feet, squeezes the potato and takes small bites with his little soft mouth. He finishes eating, throws one hand up in the Nazi salute, takes on Hitler's face. Then his face softens, a benevolent Hitler. "Little Jews," he says in a wheedling tone, "what do you want? A barber shop of your own, Max? You deserve it for your loyalty to the fatherland. Find your mother and father? I'm looking all over pigland for them. Don't worry. I misplaced them but you'll soon have them back. The heavyweight championship, Berchik? I'll get it for you—just promise to stay out of the ring. Wrestle herring barrels, tree trunks—but stay out of the ring." He turns toward Kaplan who is lying outstretched, eyes closed. His voice drops. I can barely hear, "Nothing for you, Kaplan," and louder, "and for myself—I want nothing—nothing—just your good will and a good word in heaven when you arrive. It will be soon. Tell them about me up there. I'm not as bad as they say."

I like *Othello* better, but it's been his longest speech in months. That's something.

The cold cuts as we walk into the woods. We wear

every spare bit of clothing plus heavy felt overcoats and warm hats. I slip on the ice tracks. Yesterday, Dmitri and two helpers carted barrels of water and spilled them along the road to make two ice tracks for the sleighs that would soon be used to drag the timber out of the forest. All the men peel off to their work areas, but Berchik and I must follow Dmitri farther into the timber. On we walk, the only sound the crunch of our boots on the hard-crusted snow. Then Dmitri points to a tangle of fallen trees that blocks our path. "Clear these," he says. "There is cut-down timber beyond and the sleighs can't get through. Watch out for spring-trees."

The pile of criss-crossed logs and brush towers four times Berchik's height. We chop at the edges with hand axes. Then on either end of the two-handed saw, we cut a fir that projects from the pile like a mast from a shipwreck. My head is down, the ice melts from my mustache and I suck the salty water into my mouth. Berchik's breath steams like a locomotive.

I begin prying a small tree from the heap. It comes out easily then snags. Berchik leans on his axe. "What goes on in the woods, Max, on haircut day?"

"Mind your own business, dummox. I dig for acorns and roots." Turning my back on him, I cradle the trunk in my arms and digging in with my feet, leaning forward, I heave and strain. Berchik's axe rings again.

I drive my right hip against the trunk and push. A rumbling sound. I drop the trunk, begin to run and trip over the axe handle; twist to avoid the blade and land on my back. As I raise my arm to protect my face, the forest rains branches upon me.

I awaken bedded in straw. A giant figure wavers before my eyes. I close them. My head hammers. I try to sit up. Fall back. Berchik is on his knees, next to me. "I thought you'd never wake up, little Max." He clasps my hand. "Get well, rest, little barber. I'll miss the potatoes you find in the woods. Without you, I'll starve to death." I lie still. I drift off into warm, round arms. I hear the door open and shut.

Berchik brings the oatmeal laced with honey each morning. Later in the day, Sofia brings warm water in a basin and soap; sometimes an apple or two or black bread and honey. My vision blurred one day, I couldn't see—I thought Velvel was staring at me as if he'd like to wrest the bowl from my hand.

After the nurse from the barracks hospital left, I finally asked Berchik, "Where is he?"

"While you were sick, they asked for volunteers to go to Alma Ata. They said it's warm there. Only two hundred miles from China and far, far to the south. Velvel heard there was plenty of food there. He said he was sorry to leave us. But he had nothing left to sell. He sold his suitcase for a hunk of sausage and his overcoat for a pint of vodka."

"You mean, he left without his overcoat?"

"Yes! I told you. He sold it."

"He'll freeze—he'll—"

"I couldn't stop him."

"You didn't go?"

Berchik shrugs, then drops to one knee and rearranges the blanket over my feet. "I'm here and the pregnant bride and her husband—they stayed. Kaplan's in the hospital. He refused to get up one day. I don't know how long they'll feed him. Most of the others—gone."

That night, I walk outside. The moon, a thin sliver in the sky. I mustn't lie abed any longer, even to avoid the timber cutting. I pace in one direction 978 paces, turn left, pace 640 paces, pass the road back to the railroad station, pass the road into the forest, pass the road to the lake where the logs are stored.

I work at light duty with the women, clearing brush around the camp boundaries. A Jewish man-child is born. Our first. Now for several days, the teams haul the heavy logs on sleds along the frozen track. Some time, far off, I am told, they'll be turned into rifle stocks. Down the hill to the lake, the logs are laid to rest until the spring thaw. The green fence grows higher, 978 by 640 is my world. Nothing marks the days.

We get lamb in the soup one day, almost a stew. The work day starts earlier, ends earlier. Berchik, just to annoy me, repeats, it's not safe here. He has a new partner in the wood hauling, the wizened old-timer who has survived everything.

It starts snowing again at dinner time. Over the ever-present soup, Berchik speaks with new authori-ty. "If the storm continues, no work, and we can do it tomorrow." The old-timer casts a side glance at the snow piling up on the outer windowsill. He winks and nods twice.

I walk next to Berchik, head down, into the pelting snow. He pulls the scarf away from his mouth, grips my arm, "Tomorrow, we're making a *bris*."

"Where?"

"Sofia will lend us her room. The storm on the

seventh day is a sign. Tomorrow's the eighth day after Shlomo's birth."

"Good. Walk faster. And who'll do the circumcision?"

"Max, the barber!"

"Like hell, I will. I can't. Never did one."

"Remember your first haircut. There's always a first time."

"Stop squeezing my arm, you ox."

"By my beard, you'll do it. We chose you."

In our room, I light the lantern, then take out the drawstring bag that contains my razor, soap, and whetstone. Snow has drifted through the chinks in the logs in one corner. Berchik sits on a stool, arms folded, watching.

I take out my pocket knife and the razor, open them, and place them on the table near the whetstone. The knife is dull and rusty. I try to recall every detail of the only circumcision that I've witnessed. An ice pellet hits the back of my neck. I spin around and see Berchik's arm poised to throw another. He grins, drops it, and picks up handfuls of straw and begins plugging the gaps between the logs.

I turn back to my tools and heft the razor. I trust it. I hone the edge carefully on the whetstone. I run the blade across my left, middle nail.

I awaken, feel the warmth of Sofia's early fire seeping into our end of the stove. I hear the clank of a pot. Three raps on the stove, then two more, and I struggle to my feet, shake sleeping Berchik who sits up instantly. We put on our greatcoats and with

Berchik holding my arm like a jailer, we march next door and enter Sofia's place.

The groom, wearing a new, black embroidered skull cap, stands next to his bride. A black band of sweat encircles his forehead. She cradles a bundle in her arms. A kerchief binds her head and chestnut hair curls around the edges. Her black eyes dart at me, then she looks down again at her son. A devout woman, I've been told, but she's abandoned the old practice of being shorn bald by her husband. I don't deny it: I want her for myself.

The walls here, as bare as ours, but there are four stools and a huge wooden bed near the stove, covered with an orange cloth. Kafchinski and his two boys stand in a stiff line before the bed. Sofia drapes a white towel over a small table in the corner, between stove and bed.

Berchik takes our two cups from his pocket and places them on the larger table among an assortment of cups and glasses. A bottle of clear vodka stands like a guest of honor in the midst of the cups.

"Get the vodka ready," I say, and Sofia bustles over from the stove and begins to fill a glass.

"No, no, not for me! For the child, later," and I point to the swaddled bundle, "to stop his crying. And the bandage is ready? Must I think of everything?" No point in demanding a *minyan*, the ten men that are needed for a real ceremony. No rabbi or proper *mohel*; a barber to do the circumcision.

I slip off my coat from one arm and take out the razor, wrapped in a clean white rag. Kafchinski rushes to my side and helps me remove the other sleeve. I flip the razor open, close it, and slip it rewrapped into my vest pocket. Sofia pats my arm and hands me a cup of steaming tea. She fills the other mugs and we all stand around, smacking our lips and sipping tea.

The door opens and in come Dmitri and the old-timer who hates work. Dmitri polishes his steamed-up glasses between thumb and forefinger of his glove. He takes the *makhorka* from one pocket and a sheet of *Izvestia* from the other and begins an assembly line of cigarette rolling on the table. When he starts handing them out, the old-timer takes one and lays it back on the table. "We can smoke later. Let's begin. Quickly. It will be light soon."

The mother unwraps the boy and places him on the table near the stove. He lies quiet, the little plucked chicken, just kicks his legs in slow motion.

"Berchik," I say, "go stand at the little one's feet and hold his ankles, gently, don't break them— unless," and I glance at the sweating father. He says, "Please, not me."

The old one is praying. I don't understand the Hebrew words. Except the Lord our God, the Lord is One, and I don't believe this. I'll never believe it. "Wake up, Max," I hear from far off as Berchik stands before the child, like a forest giant, his hands poised delicately above the baby's ankles.

The prayers stop. In a dream, I flip open the razor, close it again to shield the blade from the child's eyes and walk toward the altar.

The *mohel* cuts with one swift movement. I turn my head away, stare at the frosted, black window, waiting for the blue sky to appear. The baby cries.

The warm dressing is in my hand. I wrap his smallness. The baby yowls. Sofia appears with a rag dipped in wine, where did she find it, and she holds the red rag to the man-child's lips.

The child gasps, sobs, hiccups—then stops crying—the little fool.

TWO

"To work is to die," the Jewish tinsmith from Lodz, who takes us into his house says. "You'll need a work permit, go to the Alma Ata authorities in City Hall, get one; and jobs, there is plenty of work but one can't live on what we earn." He fingers the lapel of my father's overcoat. "And sell your Siberian greatcoats in the bazaar. You won't need them here." So my father, sister Marian and her husband Piotr, little Genia, and I are permitted to sleep in his shop, but must clear out, into the streets, early in the morning when the tinsmith starts repairing pails, washtubs, cleaning samovars.

Armed with my barber's tools in a leather bag, I am the first to get work in the barber shop in the railway station. A Kiev man is in charge. The others: a Vilna refugee and nine girl barbers. I work next to a Russian girl who bumps me with her big hips until I am black and blue from the bumping. They are big, these Russian girls, have no men, and need lots of room to give haircuts. Once I cut a man I am shaving, so hard am I bumped. My pay: nothing. Seventy-five roubles for a week's work.

Father, who owned three teams in Zamoscz—the Germans took everything—finds work as a teamster, another hundred roubles a week. Ration cards for everything: stand in long lines for a kilo of bread daily and meat, candy, fish, sugar once a month. Genia takes all our cards and the shopkeepers tear off the slips. We can't exist: kilo of bread, three hundred roubles; sugar, five hundred roubles; meat, six hundred roubles. And our tinsmith friend from Lodz says, "It's crowded here, two weeks you are guests, it's time to find a place of your own."

Father looks for *landsman* from Zamoscz, but the few he can locate are still living out of doors in the large park near the railway station.

A few days later, a husky young Kazakh seats himself in my barber's chair. I carry a pail of hot water from the free hot water spout outside the station and begin to soap and wash his head.

"Fool," my boss says, "take another customer—a Russian. Let the tribesmen wash their own filthy heads."

I towel the Kazakh's head, lather his black hair and begin to shave him bald.

"You are the first foreign barber who ever washed my head," he says in good Russian.

Between careful strokes I tell him, "We have just arrived from Siberia. Five of us. No roof over our heads." I wipe his head with a damp towel. "Do you know anyone who . . ."

He stares into me through narrow brown eyes. Unlike us, only a few hairs on his yellow-brown cheeks. "My father has a small house, a shepherd's hut. We no longer use it." He gets up, slips on his sheepskin jacket. I hand him his tall hat, fringed with fur and covered with purple silk.

"When can we look at it? Where is it?"

"Follow the Abay Prospect, off Lenin Street, all the way until the cobblestones turn to dirt, then past a small bazaar, open fields, and a village of nine houses, ours is the last of three on the left. Ask for Janim Batir."

I drag buckets of water from the stream and we wash down the walls of the hut. I find my Siberian work gloves and tie branches together to make crude brooms to sweep the hard packed dirt floor. Janim gallops across the field carrying a loaf of white bread. He hands it to Genia and rides off. Father scolds her for not inviting him to eat with us. I build up the collapsed fireplace with a few rocks and with camel dung and small branches, I start a fire. Seated on the earth, outside our new home, we have our first meal of tea, Kazakh bread, dried curd, and big red apples with yellow stripes, like no apples I've ever seen before.

I am forever chasing Janim's donkey away from our house. He returns to rub his backside against the corner of the house and begins to wear a hole through the clay wall. I fix the corner with clay and still he comes back. So I finally fasten some thorny branches around his favorite corner, and then he leaves the house alone.

Genia washes clothes for all of us. She sets out buckets in the sun, and in two hours, the water is warm. When she doesn't have family clothing to wash, she washes her body. I rig a screen for her in the rear of the hut, and there I can see her white feet under the cloth she drapes around herself. She cannot stop washing. She grows cleaner and her skin becomes whiter, then tans a golden color. Her hair turns lighter and glints in the sun, only her small feet remain milk white.

One day, she goes to the bazaar wearing an old blue dress. Too small for her now; all of her strains against it. She comes home soon, holding the front of the dress to her breasts, half running, stumbling, holding herself. The sun has burned the back of the dress brown and it fell apart and peeled from her back. She changes her dress, sets out two buckets to warm in the sun, to wash once again.

Five people in a twelve-by-twelve-feet hut. Piotr, still limping from the badly set ankle bone, is away for long spells, and when he returns, I sleep out of doors. Once I awaken and two of Batir's camels are joined, rump to rump and pumping away. The moon outlines their single brown humps: they sway, stamp the earth, push back and forth. In the hut, Genia must hear Piotr and Marian under their blanket. In the morning, the husband is gone, leaving dirty clothes behind for Genia to wash.

Marian, dark like a Kazakh, is the only one of us whose body is still clothed with fat. I think she and the husband eat secretly, away from the hut or under the blanket at night. Genia finds an apricot while sweeping the dirt floor one morning and pops it into her mouth.

She bears strong, healthy fat, my older sister. In Siberia, she always cut more than her quota of brush. She gets work loading sugar beets, steering her wheelbarrow up a plank and from a high platform, dumps the beets into a railway car. The Kazakhs working alongside peer under her skirt, or so she says, while she is aloft. She carries home long white sugar beets and puts them in the fireplace with their yellow-flecked skins, then slices them and we eat it when we are short of bread. Too sweet for me and gives me gas pains, but Genia likes it. And still Marian says we can't manage and asks for more money for household food.

With Marian's few roubles (I'm sure she's holding back money) and my wages added to my father's, we still can't buy enough to eat. I take two old shirts scrubbed clean by Genia to the bazaar and wander about looking for a trade. A Tatar woman squats down in the gutter, hoists her long pink skirts and a stream of urine flows between the cobblestones. I pass dark-skinned Kazakh women in red and green brocade vests carrying bundles, Uzbeks in little caps like our yarmulkes, with moon designs on the edges.

I eat with my eyes: the white cheeses they make from sour milk, dried lamb and dried fish hung from wires, smell the flat loaves of white bread.

At the edge of the bazaar, I start to turn back for another look when I hear, *"Landsman, landsman,"* and I am embraced by strong arms, squeezing the breath out of me. Berchik lifts me off the ground. I never expected to see him again when he left the logging camp before me. "Put me down, tree top!"

"Cutting any more *shmeckeles*, Maxele?"

"Let go, Berchik," I yank his beard, "or I'll cut yours off." He loosens his grip. I grab for his nuts. He blocks me with two hands and I clout him, a light one, on the head. "How does one live here, Berchik? The wages . . ."

"Trading, buying, and selling. I work in a bakery now." A Kazakh rider lopes by and turns his head to stare at us through slanty Mongol eyes. The rider kicks his horse to a gallop and Berchik spits after him.

"Why spit at him, Berchik?" I tell him about the good Kazakh neighbors who let us use their hut.

Berchik grinds the spit with his boot heel. "Let's not argue, old friend," and he grasps my elbow and draws me across the path. We sit in the shade of a tree. "Here, take this," and he reaches inside his shirt, and takes from under his armpit a ball of dough. It is streaked with dirt. He presses it into my hand. I start to hand over the two shirts. "No, keep them. How could I fit into your shirts, little Max? Have you heard any news about the family? Marian? And little Genia?"

"I found them in Alma Ata. They were in another camp. Mama's dead."

Berchik looks sad, then brightens. "How's Genia? What a pretty girl."

"Genia's shaken off a Siberian cough. Almost a woman now."

"Never go into one of their houses, Max, if the Kazakh man isn't at home. Call from outside. Plenty of Russian girls who will lie down in the fields. Just for fun. Remember your Polish one, Sofia. You pumped her in the woods, in the storeroom . . ."

"And out came oatmeal laced with honey. Without her, I'd have starved to death."

"Look there, Max." He taps my shoulder. "That broad fellow with the cap."

"Who is he? One of us?"

"A *Galicianer* and a pickpocket. Dov, he is called, King of Thieves. See how he mixes with the crowd. Walks on cat feet for a big man."

"A *goniff*? What does he steal?"

"Nothing, everything. One man pushes another. The big man is there. You should see how he can cut out a jacket pocket with a razor. A champion! And I've found a Russian-Jewish girl from Leningrad," he hefts the air with his palms up, "a little past her prime, but she's grateful."

After we part, I go back into the bazaar and stop before a young Kazakh matron in a white headdress who is pushing an ammunition box tied to a tree branch. Inside, a black-haired baby sleeps. I trade with her: two shirts for a red shawl that the women wear on their heads and drape around the shoulder.

When I present the shawl to Genia, she hugs me, puts it over her head and parades around the yard. Marian looks up from the fireplace where she is pushing more sugar beets into the embers. "When we need food, you buy Genia a *sali*. Didn't you know that's the head covering for a Kazakh bride?"

"A young girl needs something pretty, Marian."

Genia runs into the house and comes out with my shaving mirror.

"Stop admiring yourself, Genia," Marian says. "Get some water."

I pick up the pail.

"Maybe you're right, Max," Marian says. "Bring your friend, Berchik, some evening. I remember him. A strong young fellow."

"Not for our sister! He's a *bullvan*. Good hearted, yes, but coarse, not half good enough for Genia. I'll get the water tonight," and I start across the field. Must remember to bring Marian a gift sometime.

I sleep on a bench with my feet resting on the stove. Marian tosses heavily on one side—Piotr gone again. My father coughs and hawks, gets up, goes outside, then I think he lies awake. Genia, can't hear her breathing, sleeps with a blanket over her head against the far wall. What does she dream about? If I open my eyes, I can look out the only window.

It rains one night, water pours through the roof onto my head. When the sun rises, I climb on the roof and look for holes. I can't find any openings.

I see Janim Batir galloping across the fields, scattering sheep before him. He stands below me, tall in the stirrups. "Our dog is gone! Have you seen any Koreans?" He seizes the knife haft at his waist. "They eat dogs! If I catch one of them. . . ." He pulls the knife half out of its leather sheath and draws his left index finger across his throat.

"No one passed by, Janim. I'd have seen them."
"Come down, Max." He leaps off his horse. "We
Kazakhs know how to keep the rain from coming
through a roof." Genia appears in the front yard, a
bucket in her hand.

Janim takes the bucket and we go into the fields,
Genia following a few steps behind. He stoops
whenever he sees a pile of horse dung and drops it
into the pail. When we go back, he takes a branch and
mixes a paste of dung and clay, adds a small amount
of water. "Now, coat the roof with this mixture," he
says to me. "When I was a small boy, we all lived here
until father built a larger house. Many is the time I
climbed the roof and did this job."

I climb up again and smear the smelly paste over
the roof. Janim mixes more paste and hands it to me.
As I climb higher, toward the smoke hole, Janim gets
on his horse, jumps to his feet, squats on the horse's
back; Genia hands him the pail and he steadies
himself and stretches until he can hand the pail over
to me.

I reach the conical top of our hut, begin working
my way down the other side, then slide off. Janim has
disappeared. I walk around to the front. He comes
from the direction of the stream, carrying two buckets
of water, Genia at his side. A handsome fellow, that
Kazakh.

Silently, side by side, we wash our hands. Genia
brings towels and cups of tea for us. "Come see our
new foal, Max," Janim says, handing his cup back to
Genia. "A beauty."

In the fields, back of Janim's house, he lifts the top
post of a small corral and inside, a plump brown mare

grazes, and the foal nuzzles against the mare's side. "It takes two to milk a mare," Janim says. "A colt to start the flow, a man to fill the pail." He picks up a bucket and speaking to the air between Genia and me, "If someone would hold the colt, steady her against the mare . . ." And Genia, who has no love for horses, steps forward boldly and presses her body against the colt. Janim kneels on one knee and strips the mare's teats. Over his shoulder, he calls, "My father loves the *kumiss*, our milk wine. He claims it is best from a mare that has newly foaled."

When we leave, he scoops up a chicken and presents it to Genia with a little bow of his head. She holds it tightly to her breast all the way home and this one, named Beryl, is the start of our flock. Beryl loves watermelon and with Shoshanna, Rachel, Sarah, Bathsheba, and one I call Marian because she tries to boss all the others, we soon have eggs to eat with our black bread, curds and dried millet. Dried millet: food for the chicken in Poland; food for humans in Alma Ata. And while Rachel becomes our most reliable layer of eggs, it is Beryl whom Genia loves above all the others.

My boss at the barber shop lets me work only two days a week and in this way, I can keep my work permit, and I begin to be a buyer and seller of underwear. Whenever I step outside the barber shop to the bazaar, I see the big pickpocket. Other Jews come up to him, whisper in his ear; like an army captain, he sends them off; this way, that way. I buy three or four pairs of underwear at the big bazaar outside the railway station and the following day, I resell the rough cotton underwear at a smaller bazaar near our home. I set aside a few roubles. Leave for the barber shop without the black bread and tea that Genia prepares at home, and on the long walk to work, I stop and buy the round loaf of white Kazakh bread from one stall for thirty roubles and at another I buy from a wrinkled Kazakh woman a jar of curdled milk, brown on top and still warm when she takes off the towels over the wicker basket and hands me the jar. She lends me a spoon and I tear off bread and spoon the curdled milk, warm and creamy into my mouth, a little guilty about eating this well, but it's so good, I can't resist.

One day, Genia brings me ten yards of green army cloth. I sell it for one thousand roubles and only afterwards ask her, "Where did you get it? Can you get any more?"

"I can't tell you his name. The man works in a factory and he is afraid. Give me two hundred roubles and he'll be satisfied."

In the following weeks, Genia provides me with more green army cloth; usually ten yards, once twenty, then ten again, and one evening when I return from the barber shop, there are two bundles of cloth on the bench, about fifty yards I'd guess, and my father takes notice. "How did you carry that cloth, Genia? It's very heavy."

"No, it's not heavy at all," she says, and steps to the bench to pick up the top bundle. She raises it to one shoulder, staggers under it, and I leap to her side and ease the bundle off her shoulder, drop it back on the bench.

That night, I celebrate our new wealth and feed all of the remaining dried millet that we cooked for ourselves to the chickens—the way it should be—in Poland, chickens ate the millet, we ate the chickens.

A good sale the following day. I suggest to father that we celebrate and kill one of the chickens for dinner. "Which one is hardly laying any more?" I ask Genia.

I think it is Beryl, the one she fondles and pets, but she quickly answers, "Sarah."

I hone my knife on the stone from my barber's kit bag. I will cut quickly, like a *shochet*, one quick cut; the animal must feel no pain. Flick, flick across the stone, a spark flies from the blade, it's shining and clean now, and I march outside to the pen in the back. Genia watches through the window. I pick up Beryl, stroke her feathers while the vain bird preens and stretches her neck, when my arm is torn from its socket. The bird flies off squawking and Genia stands in front of me, shooting fire from her eyes. "You wanted to kill my Beryl. Murderer!" and she pounds on my shoulder.

I jump back and raise a hand to ward her off. "No, no, she's one of the family. I'd never hurt her." Genia scoops up Beryl and runs into the fields.

I seize Sarah, hold her under one arm, a quick cut, blood spurts—no good—botched the job—another cut—more blood, and I throw the bird into the air out of the pen. She runs in circles, squawking, then smaller circles, then collapses on the grass.

Genia undercooks the chicken and it is tough and stringy.

Father goes to work day after day, like a horse in harness, notices nothing, until one morning, he says,

"Follow her, the little businesswoman. See where she gets that cloth."

I stick black bread in my pocket, wrap a cloth around a jar of hot tea and start out for the bazaar. One hundred feet past Janim Batir's house, I settle down at the side of the road to wait. I eat the bread, wash it down with bitter tea, forgot the sugar I like to hold in my mouth, roll a cigarette, finish it, roll another, cough, stub out cigarette and drop the unburnt tobacco in my pocket, hack and cough and can't stop coughing. No one comes along the road.

Another day, I cut into the field past the back of our hut, to a point where there is a clump of trees and the road curves here and sets out for China with no house for a long stretch. A tribesman driving a donkey, pulling a four-wheeled cart, bigger wheels in the rear, comes past my hiding place. I sit down against the trunk of a tree. Then I hear a clear voice singing, and I know without looking through the bushes, it must be Genia. She turns off the road on the far side and disappears into the brush, just before the plank bridge where the stream crosses the road. Why would she come this far, carrying a bucket, when there is the same water one hundred yards back of our house from this same stream that curves back of the woods, drops under the road, and then continues a long way until it flows into the Ili river.

I start across the road, hear fast-pounding hoof-beats, and I scramble back into the brush. Here comes Janim Batir flying along. He passes me, bent low over the roan's neck, and at the bridge, turns his horse to the right and disappears down the bank. I run across the road, slip on the incline, get up and can no longer hear the horse thrashing through the undergrowth. I almost step in fresh horseshit, skirt around it, the earth wet here, and the horse's hoofprints have filled with water. Hear voices and step carefully. Janim's horse is tethered to a tree and browsing from the leaves of the low branches. I hear splashing, laughing, and when I reach the stream, I see Genia holding up her long skirt with one hand, other hand in Janim's and walking ankle deep along the stream bed. His black boots dance alongside her white calves. Look at him, that Kazakh movie star. Rides horses and splashes my sister.

Father calls a family council. The husband-cripple, back from a trip, arrives. Marian stands behind Piotr, kneading his shoulders. Then Genia serves supper silently and retires to the corner bench near the stove. Father says, "She must stop seeing that savage." Genia turns her back on us, leans against the wall.

"You've told her, forbid her. . . ." Marian says.

"She hears me," my father says, "but we must not offend our landlord and benefactor, the Kazakh Batir."

"How will you live without the army cloth?" Marian says. "From your salary?" She steps toward me, chest outthrust. Gives me the pointed finger. "From your princely wages? And why didn't you watch over her? She's only a child!"

"Cock a doodle doo!" I answer. "Cock a doodle doo!"

"We lived before. . . ." father says.

"I have been approached by a Jew from Leningrad," Marian says, in a reasonable voice. "He offers

ten thousand roubles dowry if your son will marry
his daughter."

All eyes fasten on me.

"I didn't know my brother was so valuable,"
Marian says. "What do you say, Max? A fine bride
and . . ."

"No! I know this Leningrader. She's fat as a pig,
dark as a Kazakh. Everyone knows her. After we
married, she'd never stay home."

Now the husband-cripple speaks up. "If Max will
travel to Ili or farther, to Sary-Ozek, there is a good
chance for trade."

"In underwear!" Marian says. "Look, even now his
underwear strings are untied," and she points to the
string-ties dangling from under my left pants leg.

I bend down, can feel myself blushing, pull up my
pants and retie the string around my ankle.

"No, not underwear," the husband says. "I'll lend
him some roubles to buy flour and we'll go half on the
profits. He can pay me back from his share."

"Is it dangerous?" my father asks.

"No. I've been stopped a few times. Once twenty-
five roubles from each of the truck passengers pushed
into the militiaman's hand, and we were on our way."

"That's all?" my father says.

"The last time, they kept my flour. No one was
arrested but it is better if I'm not seen for a while."

"Max knows the way," Marian says. "If he can find
the Turkish baths in Ili, my friend Nadia saw him
there with some Litvak tramp, he can find the flour."

"I lived better alone in Siberia, cutting trees, than I
live here with my loving family. Not you Genia," and

I turn toward her. She sits on the bench, eyes closed, pretending to be asleep.

"Well, Max?" my father says.

"Of course, he'll go," Marian says.

"I'll go. The sooner, the better."

After Marian and her husband leave to visit Nadia, my father takes me by the arm and draws me outside. "Two years, we lived apart, Mendele, you in the barracks, not knowing is our son alive or dead, hundreds of miles away, in a hut smaller than this one, and colder. Remember the frost. The frozen icicles in your mustache. All that time, your mother, may she rest in peace, cried for you."

He drops his hand from my shoulder. "Your Siberians, Max. What would they say about a dusk like this?"

"If the swallows fly high, like tonight, Ruvin Chaim Schmulovicz, it means fine weather."

"And if the smoke from a chimney goes straight up . . ."

"It means frost."

"If the smoke billows?"

"It means a storm."

He grips my arm firmly above the elbow. "You'll take Genia with you on this trip to Ili."

"She's only seventeen. She'll hold me back."

"I want her away from here. She'll help carry the flour. You *will* take her."

The open truck pulls up and the Russian driver leans out the cab door. I hand him sixty roubles, help Genia climb on the back. She hasn't combed her hair or cleaned her boots. Chicken feathers stick to the side of one boot. People crowd together to make room for us. When the truck starts off, it picks up speed, then flies into a ditch and over a bump. I almost slide off the back. So I hang onto the side rail with one hand and place my other arm around Genia's shoulders. She tries to squirm away. "You spied on me, told them and made it worse. I hate you!"

I start to sort out the travelers. A family of Kazakhs with three children. Two Uzbek tribesmen in long sheepskin coats. One is chewing on some stringy dried meat. I overhear Yiddish from a group of four seated men; each of them looks as if he is wearing extra clothing for trading under his jacket. The truck jounces, throwing Genia against me, but this time she doesn't draw back. The Talgar peak, still snow covered like a sugar loaf, is left behind. The Kazakh mother takes a bone from her pocket, chews on it, passes it to her husband; he chews, hands it on to the children. The middle boy will not give it up. A word from the father and he hands it over to the youngest.

Genia shivers from the cold and wind. The morning chill still here. I drape my short coat over her. She smiles now, a tiny smile. The wind whips, but I'm warm, warm, like I'll never be cold again.

The two Uzbeks are the first to remove their heavy coats. The strong hot sun climbs higher in the blue sky. The trees that followed us from Alma Ata thin out and, after the first road tender's hut, about thirty kilometers, the earth on either side of the road grows sandier, the low growing bushes on the slopes are gray and scorched, camels browse behind a few houses at the second road tender's hut, and quickly another thirty kilometers, and while Genia nods sleepily against my chest, the third hut appears. A freight train pulls by on the right, and two kilometers before Ili, the truck stops.

I stand and climb up on the second truck rail. The driver has thrown up the hood and is tinkering underneath. "What's wrong?"

"Sit down, *boychick*," from one of the Jews. "He always stops here and waits for the train. Sometimes there are two militia waiting before Ili. Our driver likes to pass them where the train track curves and comes closer to the road. A smart muzhik, this one. The militia watch the train and don't stop him."

I hear the train. The engine creeps into sight; it's the six o'clock passenger train from Alma Ata, two hours late. The driver hops into the cab; in seconds, we're bouncing along the road and racing the train. Smoke pours from the stack, gray smoke floats over the passenger cars opposite us now; faces press against the window panes and we pass the two militia, just as the tail end of the train pulls even with our truck.

Past the one story hospital barracks on the left, on the right the railroad station with its big front porch; passengers carrying bundles are coming out front, heading for the bazaar. As the truck stops at the Turkish baths, I wonder if Marian's friend Nadia is there today.

We weave through the crowd. More donkeys wander in the streets than stray dogs in our town of Zamoscz. Genia stops in front of a stand of white grapes, yellow honey bees buzzing around them. A donkey eats spillage from the stand, mashed grapes and earth, spits out the dirt. I buy two bunches cheaply, long ones like fingers, not the round purple grapes mother bought, only before Passover, back home.

Pass a Korean fisherman, net bag filled with fish over one shoulder, more food stands, the chicken sellers, the clothing hawkers, and along a narrow aisle, I look for Medoff, the shoemaker from Kharkov. My brother-in-law, Piotr, said he could always be found near the two barber brothers from Vilna. Next to a barber shaving a Kazakh's head and another barber stropping his razor, the shoemaker hammers on a boot sole, nails between his lips.

"Piotr sent me. Where can I find the flour merchant?"

He continues hammering, nail after nail, until he takes the last nail from his mouth. "I know many Piotrs."

"Piotr with the limp, from Zamoscz."

"Go to the other end of the bazaar near the Turkish baths. You'll see an Uzbek from Sary-Ozek with a donkey and four-wheeled cart. Trade with him." Bang with his hammer on the last nail. "He'll give you the best price."

I hand Genia three hundred fifty roubles for bread and fruit and tell her to meet me at the entrance to the baths.

He drives a hard bargain this Uzbek; thirty-five hundred roubles for three sacks of flour, leaving me with one hundred fifty roubles. I sit near the sacks to wait for Genia. After a while, I drag the sacks around the corner of the baths and move into the shade. The peddlers are leaving the bazaar, stalls covered over; it will reopen at four o'clock when it starts to cool down.

Where in God's name is Genia? Can't leave our meeting place. Down the narrow path between the stalls, she runs toward me, a loaf of bread under one arm. With a glance back at the flour sacks, I run to meet her. She grabs me. "A pogrom, Max! Like Papa told us. Run, run! We'll be killed."

"Are you hurt? What happened?"

"A Ukrainian at the two barbers—knocked them down—six, seven of them, kicking the poor barber with their boots. Pushed other Jewish stalls over, attack everyone!"

Now Medoff the cobbler turns a corner, veers left to run between two stalls. "Wait here, Genia." I cut to the right and Medoff runs into my arms. I stagger back. He raises the hammer in his hand. The side of his face is scraped and bleeding, shirt torn off one shoulder. "Leave Ili, young man. Now! The Ukrainians blame us for the Russian losses around Moscow. Who else? And me a loyal party man for twenty years! One of them knocked over the barber's chair— a pushing match—then the fool barber stabbed the Ukrainian dog with his scissors. He ran away. His brother rolled under a stand to escape them. They knocked it over. Started kicking him. Then they tasted blood, went crazy. Went on a Jew hunt, like the Czarist days. My hammer saved me. Here they come!" He sticks the hammer in his waistband, turns his back as two cars filled with blue-capped militia drive by. The second car strikes an apple stand. The crowd thins and scatters before them: apples roll in the dust. A Kazakh shakes his fist at the departing car and starts to gather his apples in a wicker basket.

"By my beard," and the cobbler tugs it, "those hooligans will taste Soviet justice. But it's better to stay indoors for a few days. Go, go," and he starts to push me with both hands. "What are you standing around for?"

I run back to Genia, give her one sack, put on my jacket, stuff bread she bought in one pocket, apricots in the other, shoulder two sacks and go around to the front of the building and enter the Turkish baths.

"Where's Nadia today?" I ask the cashier sitting near the door and hand over four roubles.

"At the railway station. She'll be back soon."

I drop my sacks near the men's dressing room. Place Genia's sack on mine. "Genia, the women's side, over there. I'll knock on the partition, three times, when I want you to come out."

While I am taking off my clothes, in bustles hefty Nadia. "Back again, Max. And with a pretty girl. Is this where you bring a girlfriend for a good time?"

"My sister, Nadia. We were trading in the bazaar and . . ."

"Another sister?"

"Nadia, please. A favor." I hand over my clothes, stand naked. "Watch the sacks of flour for me out front. And for the friendship you bear my sister Marian, when the bazaar is empty, no one on the streets, call me out."

I step into the steam room. Two full bellied men sit near the stove. One bellows, "More steam!" I sit down near the door. Nadia enters carrying a bucket of water and throws it over the stones on top of the stove, sending up clouds of fresh hot steam. I rest my hands over my circumcision, sit invisible in the fog. Take the railroad back? No—they'll be watching at the station. A truck—they won't move until four or five, tires would melt now. Leave the sacks? Never!

The door opens, a hand squeezes my shoulder. I stand, knock three times on the partition to the women's side, and enter the dressing room. Nadia hands me a rough towel and a bucket of cool water. I wipe off the sweat, blot myself dry. In the anteroom, I press twenty roubles into Nadia's hand and with the cashier's eyes boring into my back, I cross to the window. The street is deserted. Genia, shining and clean, comes out of the women's side. I step out the door, look toward the bazaar. No one. One last donkey looks at me and ambles off. All quiet. Shoulder our sacks, and we step into the broiling sun. The militia will be looking for a barber. Any barber will do.

With a sack on each shoulder, I cut off the road, feet sink into the sand. Genia follows close behind. I continue cutting right, sweat trickling down my back, off my forehead, beads on the tip of my nose. Enter a narrow ditch. From here, only the roof line of the back of the hospital is visible. Walk along the ditch and then cut back to the road. I see the back of a donkey cart filled with sacks. "Faster now, Genia. Can you. . . ." But I don't wait for her and hurry to catch up with the cart. I sidle up to an old Uzbek who leads his donkey. "Will you carry our flour?" I ask him.

"For twenty roubles. But let us rest now. We'll go on later when it is cooler."

He drives the donkey off the road and we sit in the shade of the cart on tufts of dried grass. Genia tears off chunks of bread and offers a piece to the Uzbek. And three apricots. He accepts our food and reaches in a sack and gives Genia and me two strips of dried lamb. Then the Uzbek passes around a goatskin of sour milk. We drowse in the shade. When the sun moves, we slide on our bottoms around the cart, pursued by the sun, and move into the shade again.

Now our long walk begins.

One foot after the other, sometimes I count to one hundred, then lose count, one foot after the other, for hours, forever, punished by the sun, on the road— follow the bobbing gray behind of the donkey or fasten my eyes on the half moons on the Uzbek's hat.

"How much farther, Max?"

"Half way, Genia. Keep going. Think of other things. Listen. I hear the train from Ili."

Finally the road tender's hut, so we've come thirty kilometers. And we slip and slide down a hill to his shack, to water from a small stream, to a few trees surrounding his house, and blessed rest and sleep in the shade. When I get up and shake Genia awake, my jacket is damp, so it must have rained lightly during the few hours of darkness, and we're on our way.

It's downhill now and the road follows a long sweeping curve. We come to a Kazakh graveyard. Two gravediggers are slowly digging the narrow hole in which they plant the body, sitting up and arms folded. I look back and cresting the hill—a green army truck. The truck stops. A man gets out and faces the truck. "Let's get off the road," I tell the Uzbek. "In the shade, behind those tombs."

"Wait! If you see them, they can see us." He leads the donkey into the ditch alongside the road, and in this green strip, where good grass grows from the run-off from the snow-capped mountains, he lets the donkey graze. He unhitches the cart. I glance back at the hill. The truck driver is not in sight and the truck stands poised.

"Now, but do not run," he motions to us, "over here, sit facing the tombs, your backs to the road, and bow your heads."

I hear the rumble of a heavy truck pass by, scratch my head, and peer under my armpit, expecting to see a truckload of soldiers, but the rear of the truck is empty.

"*Allah Akbar*, little brother," the Uzbek says to me, "can your wife go on?"

Genia gets up, crosses the ditch and starts down the road. The donkey raises its head and follows her. The Uzbek shouts in an unknown tongue and the donkey stops. He seizes the donkey's bridle, pulls him back and hitches him to the cart. Genia continues striding down the road, does not look back. We follow.

A few more trucks pass by, but I'm afraid to flag one down and try for a ride. My other life reappears: I drift through the Siberian taiga, come to a pond surrounded by green cedars. It is ten degrees below zero. I stand, hidden in a clump of evergreens, and watch the camp nurse drop her wrapper on the snow. She walks into the icy pond, clad only in a bra and tiny pants that do not cover her navel. Her belly button winks at me, until I'm dizzy, staring into the sun, sears my eyes—stop—close my eyes—a red

haze—open them. I see a young woman—strength in
every line of her—from thin back to hips—to dust-
covered black boots.

When the Uzbek comes out of the next road
tender's hut, he says, "The Russians are looking for a
barber, not for a young man and his wife. Now let us
sleep again through the heat of the sun."

It is dark when we reach our father's house. He
rises from his place on the floor, takes Genia's sack,
then lifts the sacks from my shoulders and embraces
me. "Must sleep now, father. We'll talk in the
morning." I sink down to the floor, stretch out. I
awaken later to find a blanket tucked around me.
And someone has removed my boots. Sun streams
through the window. I hear Marian, my father. Close
my eyes again. An argument? I drift off.

When I finally get up, I hear Genia singing and the
sounds of her washing out front. I look in the corner
for the flour sacks. Gone. At the door, I call out,
"Genia, don't spill the pails. Leave the water for me."

She kicks one over, leaves the other. I wash my face
in her rinse water, then propping my hand mirror on
the table, between two rocks, I quickly shave myself
clean. Lather my mustache, and with a few strokes of
the razor the Siberian mustache is gone. I go in to get
my boots.

Genia slips out the door and starts for town. "Wait
for me, Genia. I'll go with you." She continues on her
way. Father blocks the doorway, a cup of tea in his
hand. "Better if you rest, Max. Tell me about Ili, your
trip. You still look tired."

I brush past him, boots and socks in hand, running
to catch up with my sister.

Genia walks quickly, not even turning her head when we pass Janim Batir's house. We pass the small bazaar, already closing down against the heat of the noon sun. On the street past the bazaar the vendors are drowsing, leaning against the walls of the houses.

I follow Genia into Nadia's house. I blink, adjust my eyes to the darkness and Marian, not Nadia, waddles toward me on bare feet. A strong hug, and in my ear, "You've done well, Max, providing for our little sister." Then she walks to the stove, bends down and shakes two men awake. One is the bearlike Dov, the King of the Thieves, who raises his hairy arms and yawns. The other, equally filthy, but smaller, sits up, scratches his head and combs his beard with his fingers. They stare at Genia.

"Which one do you want, Genia?" Marian says.

Both men are now sitting upright. The big pickpocket motionless; the other one stuffs his shirttails into his pants, takes a comb from his pocket and runs it through his matted head.

Genia stands like a ballerina on her left foot and points her right foot at the smaller man.

"Where did you find these two, Marian? In what dung heap?"

The big man growls. "I'll turn you into ashes and smoke."

"Who is the *shadchen*? The arranger of this circus? If father knew . . ."

The King of Thieves slowly raises his hand, points at me. "Shut up! You! If you weren't almost the brother-in-law to my best friend, I'd break your back."

"Come," and Marian takes the big thief by the

wrist, tugs, and he gets to his feet. Holding him fast, she starts to push me out the door with her other hand, and as I back out, "Let's leave those two alone. Now they are engaged and must have a lot to talk over."

She is a Kazakh princess, my sister.

They have dressed her in a red *sali* and white veil, a long pink dress and over it a brocaded blue and green vest. Her polished boot tips gleam.

I cannot see her face. I can't bear to look at the bridegroom. From across the room, I kiss her, my sister, through her white veil.

Marian has emptied Nadia's house of furniture, which is heaped in the back yard. The room is packed, shoulder to shoulder, with thieves and thieves' girlfriends and wives. All cleaned up and dressed like ordinary men. To one side, a table is piled high with cakes and cookies and bottles of vodka. Two cauldrons of soup simmer on the stove.

A dwarf pickpocket, nomad hat cocked over one eye, jumps on a bench. "Silence! Everything here has been bought with roubles. Today is our *Simcha*. On the way out, after the ceremony, I will stand in the doorway. Every pocket must be empty, not full. Woe to the pickpocket who disgraces his comrades."

In walks the rabbi, lost in his long black coat, and held upright between two thieves. Drunk! No one here owns the clothes on his back. When I see my father cross the threshold, wearing an American gangster hat, pushing his way toward the bride, smiling, trying to smile—yes, smiling—I turn and flee from the room.

At our house, I reach under the bench and take out my barber's tools. Open the sack and draw out my razor. Sitting on the dirt floor, I open it and press the flat side of the blade against my wrist. I turn the blade and draw across my wrist. Graze the skin and a thin line of blood appears. A cowardly cut. I roll down my sleeve. When I hear my father's footsteps outside, I drop the pouch with my tools into my coat pocket.

"You cut yourself, Max?" my father says.

I stand and face him. "You arranged it all—Ruvin Chaim Schmulovicz. And I helped. The bags of flour," and I point to the leftover white dust on the dirt floor, "that was my sister's dowry."

"Better marriage to a Jew than dishonor with a savage."

You're a fool and a thief, old man. Can't say these words.

"I heard about your stealing in the camp, Max. They were going to lay for you and break your legs; you stole from hunger."

I turn away, spread a shirt on the bench and begin throwing a few things on top.

"Wait, Mendele Label Schmulovicz, don't turn your back on me."

I sit on the bench, wait.

"I'm tired, Max." He sits down on the other bench, leans back against the table. "We live, others die, Max. Isn't that being a pickpocket? I steal from my boss's wagon now. Drop off a few goods in the wrong place. A man holds it for me. A little here, a little there. We are all pickpockets."

I go back to my packing. Underwear, stockings, shaving cup, and soap. Slip my knife into my coat pocket. Tie the tails of the shirt and the sleeves together. I take the bundle under my arm, skirt around my father's outstretched legs and I can hear my own voice say, in a formal way, "I leave your house."

Did I hear him say, the night is cold, take a blanket or did I imagine this? Outside, my flushed cheeks are cooled by the fresh breeze of the Kazakhstan dusk.

I walk to the road and sit down. The donkey brays and like a gray shadow, passes behind me, returning to his old home. He disappears around a corner of our hut. I follow the Siberian custom: before a long journey the friends and family of the traveler all gather and sit with him in silence, until it is time for his departure.

It grows darker and I am wrapped in darkness. It is time. I get up and walk down the road.

THREE

At lunch time, two blue-visored NKVD men, in a black car, circle the factory, never getting out of the car, looking everywhere, then ride away. No talking when they are around. I go from factory to the barracks three blocks away; soup and bread for dinner; an upper bunk three feet from the next bunk; black bread and chicory coffee, weak and tasteless for breakfast. Lunch, whatever I can scrounge to be eaten at the grinder, during the half hour break.

For a month, I sweep the floor clear of filings,

dump them into boxes and carry them to the storeroom. The metal slivers cut through my gloves and drive into my hands. I pull them out, except for one stubborn one that lodges in my palm. Then I get a promotion. A tall, bearded Tadzhik picks up my broom. The Russians import them from Tadzhikistan; some come from as far as the borders of Afghanistan to work in the factory. The Tadzhik women are light skinned and look a lot like our women. No Kazakh nomads here. They drive their flocks of sheep from one grazing place to another and are unsuited for factory work.

The Russian mechanic shows me how to ream the torpedo, grind the edges and get off the rust. The torpedo moves on conveyors overhead; the conveyor stops and two of us grab the pulley chains and lower the torpedo to the milling machine. The Tadzhik sweeps the filings and hauls them away. Up goes the torpedo, down the line, out of sight and down comes another. One day like another at the torpedo works on Tashenska Street.

One night, a foreman awakens me at one A.M. to unload sheets of metal plate that have arrived at the freight yard. I return to the barracks, bone weary, four hours later. Into bed and up in an hour to go to the works.

My grinder squeals, moans, and comes to a halt. The Russian mechanic doesn't come to fix it. Other machines are shut down. The loudspeaker blares: *Germans stalled at the gates of Moscow. Our people dig in . . . prepared to fight, street by street, General Zhukov counterattacks on 200 mile front . . . heavy blow. . . .*

"An entertainment today," the Lubliner at the next machine shouts, "all the way from Leningrad."

A miracle! After the lunch break, the line stays shut down. The black NKVD car circles the floor and halts before a platform that has been quickly erected that morning. One NKVD man helps a captain with a chestful of medals and slighter sergeant onto the stage. The captain speaks, waving his fist . . . the motherland fighting for its life . . . they fight on . . . the glorious dead . . . the invincible Red Army . . . the valiant hero-civilians who refuse to be evacuated.

I nod, chin on chest, then snap myself awake. The captain wipes sweat from neck and forehead. A few Russian mechanics applaud but the Poles and Tadzhiks remain silent. The captain puts his arm around the sergeant and introduces her as his comrade-in-arms, Sergeant Bronya.

She sweeps her cap off and black hair tumbles out. With a leap, she jumps off the platform and places one foot on the running board of the NKVD car. "I am happiest when I am close to the hero-comrades on the farms and in the factories."

I admire her black shiny boots and fine strong figure. She holds her cap at arm's length and starts to sing:

> In the trenches they sent me a present
> I'm a soldier you can see
> And 'twas pleasant receiving that present
> For someone at home thought of me.
> Was it Sonya, was it Tanya, was it Manya
> All the same, all the same
> Was it Sonya, was it Tanya, was it Manya
> All the same!

Loud applause. Rhythmic foot stamping that grows faster like a brigade of cavalry horses. When she finishes, I am not sure if she sang in Russian or Polish.

The next day I ask for two days off to visit my father. I tell the comrade in charge of recruiting that I must see him once more, before I volunteer for the Polish brigade.

My father hugs me, pushes me along into our hut. "Sit, rest, eat," and he lays a Kazakh flat bread, apples, butter, strips of lamb before me. Not a word about our last quarrel.

"I can't stand that factory, Ruvin," I say to him. "Look at my hands." I turn them palm up so he can see the gashes and cuts. "From handling the metal filings—without gloves."

"I'll get you gloves. We'll find gloves. It's nothing. You're safe there making torpedoes. What happened to your gloves? Didn't they give you gloves?"

"I sold them." I tear at a piece of dried lamb. Stuff bread into my mouth with my other hand. "You must have read in *Pravda*, Moscow is under heavy siege. Odessa has fallen, many Jews there. What will they do? And Sevastapol may be next."

"It has nothing to do with us. Our *landsleit* from Zamoscz pressed together in the gas chambers of Maidenek, pressed together like herrings in a barrel."

"That's why, father, why we must do something. The Nazis shoot us and push us into one big grave. Bodies fall every way. Sitting upright like the Kazakhs plant their dead, or feet in the air, on our backs. . . ."

"What can *you* do? The world knew and saw; made itself deaf, dumb, and blind!"

"Some Jews are ready to fight. I'm volunteering."

"Fool!" He slams his fist on the table. "The Russians treated us like criminals until they, too, were attacked by the Germans. Now our Polish government is in London, safe and sound, thousands of miles from the fighting and they want us to fight for the Russians. Don't do it, Max. You've used up one life in the Siberian camps. Don't be so ready to risk this second life."

"Ah, this food tastes good after the barracks garbage. When I knew I could get out tonight, I gave away that dishwater they call soup. I'm going out for a while."

"Where? Stop and have your tea."

"I want to see Genia." I get up from the table. "I hope that Hungarian thief, Tibor, isn't there."

"Her husband now, Max. Forget old quarrels."

"A thief."

"In Kazakhstan, the thieves become wise men, and the wise men become thieves."

I steal into our hut, hoping Father will not awaken and ask more questions. Genia has lied to me, I am sure, about life with her thief. They get along, she said. Soon she will be moving to Ili, not far from the bathhouse. The thief claimed he could do more business in the smaller bazaars of Ili. Less competition. Remember the fresh milk from the cows at Grandpa's in the country? The female cows here have horns, I answered. Will we ever go back home, she asked. This hung between us while we sipped our tea.

I lie on the floor, next to the only window, my old place. Pull a blanket over me. The night air turns chilly. I drift off. The horses clip-clopped along and the wagon swayed from side to side. My sister and I lay side by side in the hay. Father's broad back on the wagon seat. Shmulka, Baron, you know the way, little horses.

A banging in the night. I sit up, rub my eyes. The door flies open, thong and peg pulled from the frame. Two soldiers burst in. "Get up. Up! The army is waiting for you."

I stand up. "I was going to join in a few days." My father sits, back against the wall.

The taller soldier turns to the other. "That's what the big fellow said in the last house on this road."

The smaller one says, "Almost missed this one. You didn't think we'd find another on Kazakh land."

The big soldier taps my shoulder. "Get your things. With our help, you'll get to the front faster."

"All my things are at the torpedo works."

"You won't need them," from the arm tapper. "The army will give you everything. Come along. No time to lose."

I slip my knife into my belt. Look at my father. He doesn't stir. Scoop up my leather pouch with my barber's tools. I'm lucky to have taken them from my barracks.

"Hurry, hurry," and he shoves me along. I kick the door peg lying on the floor and send it flying through the doorway. Another shove and I stagger over the sill. A half dozen men carrying assorted bundles are waiting outside, guarded by two soldiers. My father appears in the doorway. He takes out his watch and presses it into my hand.

A sweet cool morning. A donkey brays. The red sun hangs in the blue sky.

I buy a loaf of bread and a jar of curdled milk from a Kazakh woman at the station, wash it down with a glass of *kumiss*. A few drops spill on my green army pants and I rub the stain with my fingertips. Rub the same cloth that I have sold in the bazaar.

The train pulls in, belching smoke, and the soldiers rush for the benches so they can stretch out at night. I lag behind, leaving father, sister, friends, and I'm in no hurry to board the train.

I climb in, open compartment doors and find all second and third row sleeping benches are taken so I drop into the nearest wooden bench. After a while, a fellow above me leans down, hand in my face. "I'm Yasha from Lvov." I shake his hand.

I doze off and sleep fitfully, head pillowed on my overcoat. I awaken, stretch and twist to unkink my neck. Yasha vaults to the floor and motions me up to his bunk. The train labors up a mountain, over a trestle, a deep gorge below. The orange sun begins to slip behind the Kirghiz mountains. I climb up and stretch out.

I awaken suddenly, sit up and bump my head on the third bunk. Look over the side and Yasha is writing a letter in a pad which he rests on my pack. The recruits, all in the same new green, are quiet. One gnaws on a strip of meat; another stuffs bread into his mouth. Polish talk, other languages. I hear no Yiddish.

In the morning, the land has turned sandy, trees sparse and twisted; the apple orchards and good pasture land of Alma Ata left far behind. We pass three conical yurts, one stripped of its felt covering, standing bare like a torn umbrella. Donkeys graze nearby. A nomad shades his eyes and watches the train go by.

I slide over the side and sit down beside Yasha. My first good look at him: a swarthy, husky fellow, older than me.

"You're a Jew," he says.

I nod.

"Have an apple, cleans the mouth."

I bite into the large, yellow-striped apple.

"Let's go into the corridor," he says, "where we can talk."

He stands close to me in the narrow passageway. "I'm from the left, Poale-Zion. And you?"

"A barber."

"Just a simple barber, that's all? I thought we could be friends."

"We are friends. Do you want a drink? It's in my pack."

"What is it?"

"Vodka."

"Too early for me. I volunteered."

"They volunteered for me."

"You heard about the trial in Ili," he says, in a lower voice.

"The Ukrainians who beat up the Jews in the bazaar?"

"Yes. You didn't know the Chief of Police in Ili was a Jew from my town of Lvov—a communist?"

A Russian soldier, wearing a pistol, walks by. The train lurches, throwing him against Yasha. I mop my forehead with my handkerchief. "Can you believe it? Snow falling around Moscow and here, we can hardly breathe in the heat."

"It was hotter—the day of the trial, in the movie house in Ili. If only you had heard the Chief of Police, how he gave it to them.

" 'You know who you attack?

" 'Jews!

" 'You know who Stalin's wife is?

" 'A Jew!

" 'You know Kaganavich, big in the party?

" 'A Jew!

" 'You know who the biggest doctors are?

" 'Jews!

" 'Verdict: to the front lines.' "

His eyes shine. A commissar, a fanatic. "You've read Karl Marx?"

"You forget. I'm only a dumb barber."

"You're not to say that." He strikes me a light blow with his shoulder. "You can learn. We're comrades. And anyone who could find his way here from Poland . . . where did you say?"

"From Zamoscz." I am relieved when a voice shouts from the front end of the car. "Chymkent, in ten minutes. We'll stop for one hour." I hope the interrogation is over.

Yasha follows me off the train. The Chymkent railway station is bigger than Alma Ata's; a huge building, brown wooden corner beams and wooden crosses decorate the gray plaster walls.

Inside, many veiled Uzbek women and men in embroidered skull caps, older bearded Uzbeks wearing turbans; dark bowlegged Kazakhs in sheepskins and their pink-and-green dressed women; a few taller Tadzhiks and a sprinkling of Europeans.

I look for Jews. Here they eat, drink, scratch their fleas, piss, shit, sleep, make love, give birth. I lost two blood-stained towels at a childbirth in Alma Ata station. The women saved the child. All the while, they waited for tickets. Sometimes after a week or two they left, never to return or they learned the only way to get a ticket was with *blat*. In Alma Ata, the full-bearded assistant to the Russian agent was in charge of *shmears*. From twelve midnight to two A.M., everyone was thrown out, the station washed down, then it started again.

I counted twenty-four barbers in the shop near the station entrance, mostly women, twice the number in our shop in Alma Ata. We enter a restaurant, sit at a long table with other soldiers, merchants. A steaming samovar is placed before us. A Russian woman pours tea. "Ever fire a gun, Yasha?"

"Only at rabbits in the forests of Galicia. I was better at setting snares. At my first shot, all the rabbits disappeared."

I sweat from the hot tea. Turn my cup upside down, so they will not pour more. "The Germans, they say, take no prisoners. They—'

"Beasts! We learn to shoot. Ride in tanks." Yasha thrusts his finger into my chest. "Ping—they die!"

"I dreamed one night that they came, with their tanks spitting fire, the dive bombers. . . ."

"They're not coming. Not this far. We go there! Push them back from the gates of Moscow, push them back into Gehenna. Come," and Yasha takes my arm, "the train musn't leave without us."

When we get back to our car, the engine is still taking on water from a hose drawn to a tap outside the station. Another train has pulled into the siding next to ours and medical orderlies are bustling in and out, carrying buckets of water and stretchers into the cars.

I hear a shout through an open window. "Come here, over here."

I walk over and Yasha follows. A man, dirty and unshaven, lies on a lower bunk. "You are Jews?" he asks.

We nod.

"Jews! Run! Fly away. Look!" And he pulls back his blanket. Wrapped stumps. Reddish-brown stained bandages.

Yasha steps in front of me and sticks his head through the window. "You need something, a drink vodka, water?"

"Jews. Run." He turns his back on us and throws one hand over his head.

The train rattles on toward Chymkent. I sit, both hands squeezing my thighs. It seems that I have been on the run for years, never stopping long enough to wonder about being afraid. The train slows, begins a slow climb up a hill. Stops. Yasha rolls a cigarette. He offers it. I take it. He rolls another. Clouds of smoke. I grab my barber's kit. "I'll look for water, Yasha; I'd feel better with a shave." I open the compartment door, into the passageway. Into the next car, then another. I continue walking until I come to a locked door. I open the right hand door a crack to the outside. Look back at the passage. No one there. Either way, it's no good, I think, swing the door wide and sit, feet dangling over the side. My barber's kit drops to the ground. Sent there by an unknown hand. I drop to the ground, close the car door. Scoop up the kit, and stooping, I run close to the train, no doors on the next three cars—freights—can't be seen, faster, must find a hole, a tree, before anyone else leaves the train. A ditch, bushes alongside. I sprint for them, ducking low, push them aside, a branch snaps like a gunshot, and I dive into the ditch. I lie on my elbows: belly, thighs, legs in the warm, muddy water.

I'm tied to my barber's kit; the loop twisted round my finger. I raise the leather bag, let the water drip off, wipe it with my handkerchief and stuff it into my shirt front. The train is passing by. It starts down the grade, car wheels screeching. I look over the edge of the ditch, part the grass while the last car crests the hill and disappears.

I climb out of the ditch and decide to follow the tracks back to Chymkent, look for a bazaar and there I'll find other Jews who can help me.

Our troop train has not traveled far and by four o'clock, I'm back in Chymkent. I lose myself in the crowd around the railroad station. I walk past the iron gate in front of the hospital, past the garden and giant poplars, and following a veiled Uzbek woman who pushes a cart with melons, I search for the bazaar.

The merchants are laying out their wares: dried fish hung from wires, piles of yellow-striped apples, heaps of melons; two Uzbek women are turning shashlik on a charcoal grate. I walk among them, sniffing the good smells.

I stop before a horse trader. A piebald horse whinnies and pulls at its stake. The trader holds the left hand of the buyer and the right hand of the seller. By bending and gripping certain fingers, the offer is made and sent through the fingers. The men sit blank-faced. One stares straight ahead; the other stares at the piebald horse. Not my father's way in Poland. The shouting and cursing that went on when my father traded. "That nag is blind in one eye." Or "Any fool can see one leg is short, how can he pull a cart?" My Kazakh friend, Janim Batir, told me this hand-holding way avoided many quarrels. The seller has no need to praise, in an exaggerated way, the many virtues of his horse; the buyer does not have to point out the horse's bad features.

I want to mount the horse and ride off. Where would I go? Then I hear a scream, "Max, Max," and I turn around and a middle-aged woman is hugging me. It's Chaya from Zamoscz. Our people, lived not far from us. My father used to transport the husband's herring barrels.

"Not so loud, Chaya," I grab her wrists. "Over here, come, we can talk better," and I lead her behind the corral, away from the traders.

"How is Yankel, Beryl? How is Shloime?" she asks me.

"Still in Siberia." Let her find out from someone else that Yankel and Beryl are buried under the snow and the other—I don't know him. I place my palm over her mouth. "I need a place to stay, a change of clothes. . . ."

"Come to our kolkhoz," she says. "It's not far."

The settlement, six poor huts, three on either side of a dirt track, some scruffy looking chickens in a pen, beaten down earth, hard-baked and crusted in Chaya's front yard, one lone apple tree, and no sign of growing vegetables or orchards that I expected to find.

"Only six Jewish families here," she says.

"Even out here, the Jews are in a ghetto. No room for you with the other comrades."

"No, that's not it. The other muzhik live nearer the fields, about a half mile farther down the road. We are on kolkhoz land, but only two of our men work for them."

"They let you stay? Why do you stay here?"

"Easier for us than in town, in Chymkent. We get vegetables, sugar beets, other stuff from the kolkhoz, leftovers of course, not part of the quota they give the soviet, and with these goods we trade in the bazaar."

Chaya pushes the wooden side door and invites me inside. A poorly fitting door and a poor place, I can see at a glance. A man rises from a stool. "Ah, Yitzhak," I greet him. I remember a round, fat barrel of a man. Now he is a scarecrow.

Then a thin girl runs in. Her skirt too short; blouse too large, with a ruffle on the front; like a lady's blouse from Warsaw. "Give Max an apple," her mother says. The girl, only a child in Siberia, looks at me shyly and slips past, out the door.

The husband coughs.

"Yitzhak has not been well, ever since we arrived here. Always cold. He sits next to the stove on the hottest days."

I keep one eye out for the girl's return.

"You can report to work to the kolkhoz foreman, a Russian, called Nicolai, tomorrow," she says. "Tell him you want to work for the Two Rivers Kolkhoz. Mostly Kazakhs there. The government is trying to turn them into farmers. They badly need able-bodied men. Also, they'll give you food. . . ."

"Excuse me, Chaya, dearest sister—that's how you feel to me." I go to the door and throw out both arms and Chaya's girl-child runs into them. She hands me an apple. I take it and the girl begins eating a second one. "Here," and I take one hundred roubles from the pouch around my waist, "take this and buy us some food."

In a short time, the girl returns with a black bread under one arm and a bucket of sour milk. The husband grabs a ladle from the stove, dips into the bucket and drinks, drinks—white whiskers gather on his beard. "I'm sorry," he says, "I'm sorry."

I lose my appetite, watching him.

When I awaken in the morning from my bench near the stove, I find an old pair of pants and shirt next to me. Shielding my nakedness under the blanket, I put them on. My green army pants and shirt lie on the table. A pot with sour milk and millet boils away on the stove.

"Do you want these clothes?" Chaya says.

"No. Bury them, burn them."

She takes a knife and cuts the seams open, strips off the buttons. "Army cloth now, can get a few roubles for it at the bazaar."

After breakfast, I walk down the road toward the kolkhoz fields. Other men are leaving their huts, hoes on shoulders and walking ahead of me. The Kazakhs in their quilted coats and wide-brimmed hats that they wear even in the summer heat; two Europeans in shirtsleeves and city shoes. I hang behind, do not want to talk to anyone. I continue through a settlement of twelve houses and at the last one, a tattered red flag hangs from a pole and in front, a burly man, a ledger open before him, sits, fumbling with cigarette paper and tobacco. I stop for a moment. Men come up to him and he motions them right or left. Now he flicks an abacus with his left hand, not looking at it. Two men go into a hut and come out bearing baskets. I rehearse Chaya's instructions and when the work chairman starts to roll a cigarette on top of his ledger, I walk up to him.

"I want to work for Two Rivers."

"Where are you from?"

"Poland, Siberia, Alma Ata."

He licks the paper, taps the cigarette on his ledger and searches his pockets for a match. Three pink stumps of fingers on his right hand, right thumb whole, index finger can't uncurl.

I dig out a match, give it to him and he strikes it on a stone on the table. Pulls in the smoke. "Work papers, let's see them."

I pull out my papers.

"What does a barber from the city want at our kolkhoz?"

"I'm tired of barbering. I want to help the Soviet war effort and gather food for the hard pressed Soviet army."

He grunts. "First you can gather stones and tear out brush. Your name?"

"Max Berkowitz."

He laboriously enters my name in the book with his maimed hand. "All right, Max the barber. Go into the shed and find a mattock. Do you know what a mattock is?" He yawns and bares two rows of shiny, steel teeth like a pike's. "Like a pickaxe on one end, flat on the other. Then go through those two fields of sugar beets, make a right turn past the apple orchard, and report to the foreman at the new field. If you can work, come back when you finish and we'll give you a food ration for supper. You can eat it here or take it where you are staying. You have a place?"

"Thank you, Comrade Commissar," I start to turn away toward the shed, "with Chaya and Yitzhak Kovalski."

"With the Jews!"

I want to hear no more.

The white sun strikes the field with blinding, white light. I cut and dig and stack brush. The commissar said "gather stones," but there are few stones. When the sun burns high overhead, two Kazakh women bring bread and tea for us. Two Uzbeks, a Pole I think, four Kazakhs—they do not speak to me and I follow them to the irrigation ditch at the edge of the field near lines of newly planted apple trees. Here, we take off our shoes, roll up our underwear and rest our feet in the water. Four nomads face the east and mumble a quick prayer. One man takes out a cucumber and munches with his bread. Others have radishes, apples, bits of dried meat. I bite into the flat, white bread. Dry. The Lithuanian? Latvian? (he did not understand me when I addressed him in the fields) rinses his cup in the ditch and hands it to me. I fill the cup with tea from the gallon can. Down it in one gulp. A good sweat breaks out on my forehead. I refill the cup, eat quickly, more tea, and return the cup with a big thank you and smile.

The others lie down in the sparse shade of the trees. The war is far away. Strange birds swoop down on the field. Pick at the earth. I dig into the earth with my finger. Sift a handful through my fingers. A white heron rises from the ditch and settles onto the steering wheel of a rusty tractor. I doze, awaken and see gray smoke in the sky. Wonder if they are burning the brush. The Kazakhs in Alma Ata who use camel dung for their fires would stack the brush and save it. I close my eyes and Genia, how she loved to wash, comes toward me, in bare feet, her skirts raised above her thighs, arms outstretched; she splashes through the drainage ditch. The workers are staring hungrily. I awaken with a start. A shout from across the fields. The men struggle to their feet and we go back to tearing out brush. At the end of the day, I am given half a black bread and a cabbage. I bring it back to Chaya's hut and she cooks the cabbage while I cut the bread into four equal pieces. I roll up in my blanket and sleep outside under the apple tree.

After six days, a rest day. It's not Saturday or Sunday, just a day. I ask Chaya to tell the others that today, I will cut hair. I drag the bench outside, sharpen my scissors on my whetstone and start with Yitzhak. Snip-snip go the scissors. His black matted head takes shape, hair falls on the rag I've placed around his neck and soon I have three other customers waiting nearby. Chaya, hands folded on her bosom, looks pleased. She told me this was the first time her husband had left the shelter of the stove in a month. One customer leaves ten roubles, another two bunches of carrots, another a plain hard cake. I turn everything over to Chaya for my board. Four others are now waiting.

The fourth man wants a shave too. He will wait, he says, and Chaya's girl runs inside to put up hot water. Another haircut, now my comb flies and the scissors sing.

I hone my razor, lay it aside and motion the man who wants the shave to the bench. In the distance, I can hear shouts and yelling. I lather my customer with soap and hot water, stroke the left side of his face. Pull down the skin under his jawbone. The yelling grows louder and coming up the road, a dozen Kolkhozniks waving hoes, cutting the air with sickles—the shouts are angry and they turn in toward our house. Another pogrom!

I look around. The Jewish baker opens his door and closes it. "Run into the house, Chaya. Take the child." The Jewish drover for the kolkhoz has slipped away. I turn to face the hooligans, razor in hand.

My customer gets up, pulls off the cloth around his neck. "Sit down, Mr. Half-a-Shave," and I press him back onto the bench. "No one leaves here with half a shave."

The wolf pack draws closer. Nicolai, clashing his steel teeth, says, "The dogs from the north have cut off our water." His finger stumps blush with rage.

"They've dammed the canal—our ditch—to steal more water for themselves."

"We'll kill the bastards," from a young Komsomol, who buries his scythe into the apple tree. A ring of silent Kazakhs around me.

"Are you coming?" Nicolai says.

"Does Comrade Yanakov know what you're doing?" I say.

"He'd call a meeting first," the Komsomol says, pulling out his scythe, waving it over his head. "He'd appoint a delegation while the crops all died."

Two of them crowd me on either side. I start to shave the right side of my customer's face. My arm is jostled—blood runs down his jaw. The two grab me under each arm. "Take your razor, Max," one says. "We'll have work for you soon enough."

They start to move off at a fast clip, almost a run. I have no choice so I close the razor and between the two who begin to trot, each one grasping an arm, I run along with them. I glance back—the customer holds a bloody rag to his jaw. I stumble, a hand steadies me and in a ragged file, we turn away from the houses, cross the road, run through the brush, slosh through a ditch, now muddy and drying up quickly, out of it and up the aisle of the orchard, emerge on the other side, through a field of sugar beets, kicking up dust as we run. All are breathing heavily. I'm still carrying the razor in my clenched fist. Drop it into my pocket. The vein in my neck pounds.

We have fallen into a rough formation by two's. Now we are marching through a rough field, scattering the grazing sheep. Another ditch. Feet sucked into the mud. I trip on the far bank. The kolkhozniks have settled into a steady, fast walk, weapons on their shoulders. We follow the bank of the main irrigation canal. Smaller ditches run off from this one on either side. A parched wind rises from the east. We trail Nicolai up a rise in the field, away from the canal, cross another field heading for a windbreak at the crest. Nicolai pulls ahead, halts us with a hand motion, drops his flail and gets down on all fours. He crawls the last few yards and peers through the thicket. He calls us to him and we crowd around, on our knees, like puppets at a fair.

"There are four of them," he says. "With shovels. Gave them a good lesson last time. Remember?" The band nods their heads. "We're ten." He looks at his watch. "You—Elisha—fire-eater, take four men. Go around that way," he points and "head them off. We'll give you a ten minute start and then walk slowly toward them."

Elisha stands, taps four of the squatting men. "Come!"

"Don't be seen. And don't start anything until we move toward them. Remember! Wait until the last moment before you attack."

Elisha's band moves off and are soon out of sight.

"Now we can rest," and Nicolai rolls over on his back, hand shading his eyes from the sun.

I sit with the three others. Nicolai opens his eyes and looks at his watch. My jailer says, "What if they have a gun?"

Nicolai closes his eyes. "No gun. I did not see a gun."

"There are only four. . . ."

"If Nicolai says no gun. . . ."

Ten minutes become ten hours. Better if I'd stayed in the army. It's not my fight. I have no quarrel with those men.

Nicolai rolls over, gets to his feet. "Let's go. Walk slowly like you are going to the fields."

My jailer starts to push through the bushes. "No, not here." Nicolai grabs his arm and pulls him back. "We're a work party. Why push through here?" He slides down the small hill and begins to walk to the left where the ground levels, then cuts into the field. We follow.

Nicolai and my guard walk in front, three of us bring up the rear. So slowly. My guard spits over his left shoulder for luck. I wipe the glob from my forehead. We draw nearer. The three men are smoking, sitting on the ground; two backs are turned. Closer. Where is the fourth? Shovels lie near them.

One man looks up. He waves at us. Suddenly, the three men are on their feet, grab the shovels and set off at a run. The fourth man appears from a grove, leading four horses.

"After them!" We begin to run. I trail behind, sink to the ground. No one looks around. I turn about and head back. Reach the windbreak and crash through. Roll down the slope on the other side and head for the Jewish huts. Reach the path and turn in at Chaya's. The bench under the apple tree is gone. All doors are shut. I hammer on Chaya's door. She opens it a crack. Throws it wide. I rush in. Embrace her.

"Chaya, dear one, how can I thank you? I must go!" I grab my leather barber's pouch, drop the razor inside. Feel the money pinned to my waistband.

"Where will you hide?" she says. "Take a blanket, a hat. The sun will kill you."

I kiss her, a good fat smack, full on the lips. Go to the door, look out. She's hanging on one arm. "Look for the fat conductor," she says. "She has a gold tooth." I brush her off and I'm out the door heading for Chymkent.

After two hours of steady walking, I'm back in Chymkent. I pull out my father's watch. The crystal is cracked. It must have happened during the chase. It's three P.M.

In the crowded station, I peer into the restaurant. Nothing to eat since the morning. Too many recruits in green uniforms sipping tea. Families sit in semicircles eating, bundles lying near them. I stop counting the line at the ticket office when I reach one hundred and the line grows as I count. A dark woman conductor comes out of the ticket office. She stops to talk to a brawny woman stoker; smudged face and black, muscular arms. If she would only smile, I could look at her mouth. Then she goes outside, walks along the siding and ducks into a small booth. Picks up a phone. I look for gold teeth. The train comes in from Dzhambul. Passengers pour out. Others push and shove to get on. A bundle falls and clothing scatters; a melon rolls onto the tracks. I decide the one in the booth is too thin, not my savior. I go to a stand and buy a *Pravda* and a glass of horsemilk. They say after you drink horsemilk, the

shmuck will stand up. I've no use for it now. At
another stall, I buy a handful of potatoes for fifty
roubles. Little ones like peanuts. There she is! I'm
sure it's her. A rump like a shelf. A man is talking to
her earnestly, begging. She pushes him out of the
way. I stuff the potatoes in my pocket and head to cut
her off. Fumble for the roubles in my money belt.

"Conductor. Star of the desert. I must get to Alma
Ata."

She rubs thumb on forefinger.

I press two hundred roubles into her right hand.
"The ticket office is back there," she gestures with her
thumb. Then she puts the money between her
breasts.

"My father is dying. I must get home."

"Come back in two hours. Bring two hundred
more roubles. I'll see what I can do."

"Where can I find you?"

Her mouth opens in a yawn; two gold teeth gleam.
"Also, bring pickles, vodka, and bread." She looks
me up and down as if I'm part of her meal.

I get the vodka and black bread, but can't find her
pickles. In a darker corner of the station, I sit, back
against the wall, and count my roubles. Two hundred
for the conductor, leaves me little left. I'm afraid to
leave the station for the bazaar to look for pickles. So I
go out again with my gifts and sit down to wait.

The train comes from the west, from Tashkent. The
crowd surges forward. I push past a woman carrying
a chicken; a man gives me a swift elbow in the
stomach, I step on his heels, he turns around, two
others push against him, up he goes, then two more,
then the chicken lady, all waving their tickets and I'm

aboard. The conductor shoves me to one side, "Wait here," and I stand near her while passengers hurry down the aisle, throwing doors open and disappearing inside.

"Follow me," she says, and I follow her rolling buttocks to the end of the car. She throws a door open, pushes me inside. Follows me, her hand out. She counts the roubles I give her. "Stay here. Don't wander around and don't open the door."

The tiny compartment has two wooden bunks, folded back above her bunk. Clothes hang from two hooks. A slop pail in one corner and it stinks of urine and garlic. I pull down one bunk, climb in and pull a blanket over me.

After a while, she returns. I pretend to be asleep. She strikes the bunkpost with her fist. "Come down. Time to eat."

I slip down to her bed, sit next to her and hand over the vodka and bread.

"No pickles? How can I drink vodka without pickles?"

I don't answer. She pokes me in the ribs with her finger.

"I had no time, couldn't find any in the station." I uncork the bottle. "Have the first drink."

She takes a swig. Then tears off the heel of the bread and stuffs it into her mouth. "Two years on this run, back and forth, nothing to do. The real men are all in the army."

"You'll be rid of me in Ili."

"I only promised to take you to Alma Ata. Who are you? A thief, a deserter. No don't tell me. I don't want to know." She passes the bottle. I take a swig, tear off a piece of bread. We pass the bottle back and forth.

"I had a boyfriend in Moscow. He and I once stayed on line a whole day to buy a bed and mattress. They ran out of mattresses. We could have gotten married, but I wouldn't live with his babushka, an old witch, his mother and three others. The army took him. Here, let me show you his picture." She reaches under the bunk and pulls out a basket. Rummages inside, and draws out a brown faded photograph.

I examine it. A man in tie and jacket with two young women on either side.

"He and I once stayed on line three hours for a roller coaster ride. Did you ever . . . a wonderful day."

She points to the picture on my lap. "That's me." A knock on the door. "Come back later," she shouts. "I'm tired." Three raps, two more. Repeated. She gets up, goes to the door. "Tomorrow! Don't bother me now."

If only I had a gift for her, a scarf—anything. I could offer to trim her hair. No . . . better not let on that I'm a barber.

She returns to the bunk. "You're a Jew? You speak a good Russian with a funny accent." She puts her palm over my lips. "No, don't tell me. I don't care." Then she reaches under her bunk again and comes up with a basket of strawberries. "Help yourself." I take one. "No, really, take what you want." She picks up a berry and pushes it toward my lips. "Open." Pops it into my mouth. The berries, soft and overripe, are soon gone. She yawns and runs her red tongue over her gold teeth and around the inside of her mouth.

I get up. "You're tired," and I squeeze her heavy shoulders. I step on her bunk, vault into mine and strike my head on the third bunk, a glancing blow. Like the train, returning to Alma Ata, my life travels backwards.

> *Under Mendele's cradle*
> *there lies a golden kid*
> *the kid travels to . . .*
> *raisins with almonds*
> *raisins with almonds . . .*
> *sleep my little one, sleep.*

I close my eyes. I wonder how old the picture was that she showed me. A young girl then, not stout . . . when . . . now she must be at least . . . I hear her settle into bed.

"Come down," she calls out.

I turn on my belly and ease myself down to her bed. Reach for her and grab her feet. I came down on the wrong side. I start to switch sides and we bump heads. I'm on her side now, four feet where they belong. We embrace and she smells of garlic.

I awaken when the train arrives at Alma Ata. The beauty has left our bed. Now I must wait until the passengers get off and on. I search the room for food. In the pocket of an old coat, I find one hundred roubles. Take fifty, return fifty. In another pocket, I find a piece of sausage. I wonder if my father would have the strength now to holler and denounce me for eating pig. Climbing back into the topmost bunk, I squeeze in toward the wall, cradling my kit bag, and wait for the conductor's return. I pull the blanket over me, stifling now in the late morning heat. Lie there, cursing the day I took Genia to Ili to buy flour and my father arranged her wedding behind my back.

The train slows. I jump down from the bunk. Bite into the sausage, hard as a bullet, as the train pulls into Ili station.

I duck out of the train and mingle with the passengers, following those who are headed for the bazaar. How I wish I could stop at the Turkish baths. Or visit Genia in her new home. At a stall, I buy a net bag, three loaves of bread and some apricots. Then I head for the cemetery on the far side of town, a little way out. The dirt road continues past the cemetery to a kolkhoz. After a quarter of a mile toward the kolkhoz, I change my mind, no refuge there, and I turn back and enter the European quarter of the graveyard. Wooden boards for headstones, many fallen over; others buried in sand. At one tangle of bushes, there are a dozen partly buried head boards that I can use later to make a fire. In death, the Kazakhs sleep more comfortable than we do. The Kazakh cemetery is part way up a hill, and I walk up, feet sinking into sand. Their cemetery continues over the crest of the hill and spreads out. Trunks buried in sand, chest and head above the ground; all of them have a house built over each corpse. I know from my friend, Janim, that even the poorest Kazakh manages a clay roof over his head while the wealthy ones, I pass one now, sits in a house bigger than the hut our family shared in Alma Ata. I come to a small lake, throw myself down on my belly and drink deeply. I eat the sausage and a piece of bread. Chew a few apricots. The best food that I have ever eaten. I dig a hole in the sand, fit my body to it and go to sleep.

For three days, I sleep in the scrub in the daytime and wander about at night. I swim in the lake in the moonlight. In the old days, after I finished cleaning my father's stables, I used to run off and swim in a nearby lake to get the manure stink off my body. On a dare, I once swam the Wiepriz near Krasnystav. I wash my clothes and dry them on the bushes in the hot sun. When a rider or cart comes along the road leading to the kolkhoz, I hide in the brush. I run out of food. A big pike chases the smaller fish. I need tea, a fishhook, more matches, bread.

I climb the hill to the Kazakh cemetery and walk along the crest, skulking behind the tombs, watchful, hiding if I see a burial party. At the end of the cemetery, I cut across a fallow field and head for a grove of trees. Now I am in kolkhoz land. Beyond the trees, a field is planted in carrots, another in sugar beets. Food for the taking. Three workers come into the field. One looks toward the trees. I think he has seen me and I fade away, climb back up the hill, hear a shout, do not turn and I'm back among the dead. Can I find my way back there in the dark?

With a hook and line, I could catch the marinka, delicious cut open and fried in its own fat. We used to buy them from the Koreans and after we opened them, bury the egg roe—poisonous to Genia's chickens. Or a carp; it could feed me for a week.

Another day. Colder tonight and a short rain that beats into the brush, awakens me and I decide—I must leave. I walk out to the road and head for Ili. No one about. A dark shape crosses my path. Another. A herd of black-faced sheep. A small yellow dog runs after me, yapping at my heels. I pick up a stone and throw it. He yelps and runs away.

I turn into my sister's street. Start to knock on the door. I'm not sure it's the right house, so I go back to the beginning of the street and count again, and at the sixth house, I turn in.

I tap on the door. I knock again, shivering in my damp clothes.

"Who is there?"

"Max."

The door is thrown open. I embrace her. She pulls me inside; lights the lamp. She throws herself at me. I can feel her against me, big with child.

"Max, Max. What are you doing here? A leave already?"

"I left. Can you make some tea?"

"You're not in uniform."

"I don't need it anymore. Do you have any food? Where's Tibor?"

She starts the fire in the clay oven. Over her shoulder, "He's gone." Then she latches the door.

"You're carrying his child."

"Who else's, Max. He's not so bad. He's trading in Sary-Ozek. When he holds me, Max, I feel safe. But I know I'm not safe. We can never be safe until we return home."

"Poland is a slaughterhouse!"

From a shelf, she takes down our old samovar. I remember how I used to scour and polish it until it gleamed. She's bigger in the rear, losing her shape already.

"And then," she says, "people will act better, like

their real selves. And everything will be different. Eat now, we'll talk later." She lays out bread, curds, a piece of herring. I gobble the food. She pours more tea. I drink a second cup, a third, can't get enough. I tell her about my travels. She agrees to come to the cemetery, just before dark, in three days. She gathers a half loaf of bread, dried fish, a few apples, promises to buy a fish hook and line. I wrap the food in an old blanket. When I get up to go, I push my last roubles into her hand. Genia says, "I remember when you brought me red and green candies from the bazaar. Papa was angry."

It's getting light so I get ready to leave. "Go home to the old man. How can you live here alone?"

No answer. So I kiss her again, my little sister, and unlatch the door. I turn back. "No need to tell Tibor that I was here."

"He'd want to help you, Max."

"Don't tell him. Or Father."

Genia comes twice at dusk as she promised. With the fish-hook and line, I am able to catch a few small fish. Never a carp. I ration the bread. I scratch the days on a headboard. I build small fires, using other headboards sparingly, taking one out here, tearing out another a hundred feet away. When mourners come to the cemetery, I creep away and hide in the bushes. I hide from the gravediggers. Luckily, there is enough land left to bury every man, woman and child in Ili. More rain at night and Genia doesn't come on the ninth day. I climb the hill to the Kazakh burial ground and build a crude shelter of headboards against a clayhouse tomb. I disassemble this every morning and carry the boards down the hill. Dangerous, if the Kazakhs ever find me among their dead.

The days pass with no word from Genia. I must see her again. I lose count. I mark two days, then add three marks. I go to the edge of the cemetery every evening at dusk and watch for her.

I dream of a huge carp with green eyes. I can feed on him for weeks. When I awaken later, I think I see him following the smaller fish. He turns into an inlet with a lazy flick of his tail. I can trap him there. I can build a weir of headboards. Close him in. Fall on him. Knife him. The smaller fish are wary now and I catch nothing for days.

My sleep becomes fitful in the day time. An exhausted sleep from which I awaken unrefreshed. One day I rise earlier than usual, still in the heat of the late afternoon, and go to the lake. I take off my clothes and slip into the water. I paddle about, turn on my back and look up at the sky. Camel-clouds float by. I start for shore. Two Kazakhs stand near my clothes, hands resting on their daggers. I dive underwater, stay until my lungs are bursting, then surface and head for the far bank. Two others are standing there too—waiting. Either way. . . . I head back toward my clothes. I'll tell them about my good friend, Janim Batir. Will they know him? Tell them he'll offer sheep, horses for my safe return. I can feel the sharp dagger entering my chest. I stand up in chest-high water and slowly walk toward them. Two more stand in back, spread out. No chance to escape.

A stocky Kazakh, in a Russian cap, stabs his finger at me. "Here is your thief."

I stand still, up to my hips. Naked. A thief might have a chance. If they had seen me sleeping against their tomb—finished.

I look into the slanty eyes. Not a sign. I am condemned. I raise my head and howl like a dog. Still howling, I walk until the water reaches my ankles, then sink down and throw mud on my head. I prowl back and forth in the shallows, on hands and knees, lap water with my tongue and howl again. I stand up and walk toward them singing: *Sh'ma Israel, Adonoi Elohenu, Adonoi Echod.* I like the sound of the Hebrew. So I repeat it, chanting louder and louder. I am a Hebrew prophet. A holy man. I'll smite them down like we struck down the Philistines. If only I had the jawbone of an ass. . . .

I will not feel the blow.

I stand on dry land. They have drawn back and are talking. The leader points across the lake. No hands on dagger hilts.

The sun disappears.

I chased it away.

I close my eyes and continue chanting. I will not howl like a dog. I open my eyes and sing my own Kaddish.

A Russian appears with two other kolkhozniks. "Take that fool," he says, "to the police station in Ili. And keep your knives in their sheaths. He's either crazy or a deserter. Leave him for Soviet justice."

The cell measured two paces and a little more by four paces. A barred window over his head. Rough concrete walls. Above the window, on the right hand side, a hole in the wall. He leaped for the window edge, grasped the bars, pulled himself up and reached into the hole. He drew out a piece of garlic. Now he had garlic to rub on his stale bread.

He became a model prisoner. Traded a few matches for a needle made from a fishbone; for his last *makhorka*—some thread. He sewed his torn pants and shirt.

He tried to remember *Othello* that he had seen three times in the Moorish-looking opera house. Once with his sister, Genia . . . the taste of ice cream in the balcony . . . all the girls he had ever known . . . Sofia who fed him oatmeal in the Siberian camp . . . a little girl lived next to the bathhouse in Zamoscz. He called her Putzi since he did not remember her real name . . . the round, satin shadows in the moist heat . . . the budding breasts of the young girls . . . the shaven heads of the religious beauties . . . he cried for them . . . the plaited black hair, like the Uzbek women, loosened and shimmering down the curved back of a young matron . . . the attendant kicked him sprawling one day when he was peering through a crack in the wall while the women were taking their *mikvah* bath to get ready for the Sabbath.

Every day of the week, he married another girl. By one, he had three boys; with another, three girls. He tried not to think of the Monday and Tuesday girls on Wednesday or Thursday since he needed them to fill those days. His Friday girl turned into his sister. He pushed her away.

Then began his dreams of horses. He traded sheep for horses, camels for horses, goats for horses. He gave one hundred horses for his own marriage portion. He gave his father two teams to replace the horses stolen by the Germans. He galloped with the Kazakhs, swooping across the fields, astride a white horse; he bore down on the two leading riders in their foxskin capes, and shouldering their shaggy ponies aside, he swooped the goatskin from the ground.

He whispered into the ear of his white horse, and the animal led the herd through the bazaar and trampled the thief-husband into a bloody pulp.

A voice called out and smashed his dream.

He followed the guard down the hall, many twists, many turns, until he came to a brown door. The guard opened the door and motioned him inside.

The hanging light blinded him.

"Sit down."

He sat in the only chair under the light. Opposite, to the right of the door, a pair of black boots under a table.

He looked up—the conductress of the train! No, thank God. No. Her older sister.

"Why did you call yourself Max Berkowitz? Speak up!"

"I was afraid."

"Your name?"

"Max Label Schmulowicz."

"Your real name now. Quick!"

"That is my real name."

"You are a German spy. A Polish fascist spying for them. Here—" and she leaned across the table, shoved a writing pad toward him. "Write your confession."

He remained dumb.

"Write!"

He wagged his head from side to side. Then he stared at the shadow behind her for many minutes. For a half hour? An hour?

"Back to your cell."

He began to welcome the summons, always at night. The long walk along the corridor. He counted 555 steps. Sometimes 545. *Confess!* Silence. *Back to your cell.*

No garlic for his bread. The little scrap of garlic was gone.

Five hundred and fifty-five steps.

She stared at him. He waited for the word. Then a guard entered the room from the right, carrying a tray above his head; the man walked slowly. Max saw crossed skewers of lamb, crackling and fat dripping, a steaming bowl of soup, a mound of strawberries, apricots, a bowl of cream, a whole black bread, four onions. He smelled.

The guard walked through a door at the left.

"You are hungry," she said. "Misguided man. Eat something. Help yourself."

The guard reappeared, the tray held lower in two hands; the tray offered to him.

He froze to the chair. Sat up straighter. Thought he heard her single word—*Confess.*

The tray disappeared.

"Where do you Jews hide your gold?" she said, as she arose from behind the table, walked toward him, chest heaving—her right hand held a ring of keys, black hairs on her wrist; the hand swung in a wide arc and the keys smashed against his temple. He fell to the ground and the chair dropped across his legs.

No garlic.

Still he climbed daily to feel inside the hole . . .
lost track of the days . . . he ran from wall to wall,
touching each wall with his hand . . . he counted
each tap . . . he ran the other way . . . he grew
dizzy . . . he fell . . . he reversed directions, ran
again, back the other way . . . then he sat on the
floor . . . he sat in each corner, pushing the walls
with each hand . . . he strained at the walls . . .
moved them . . . strained again with all his might
. . . he blacked out, fainted, awakened and crawled
to another corner to push against the walls . . . he
fainted . . . he sat in the middle of the floor . . .
scratched days on the walls . . . the brown steppes
flowed by, the long train ride, scratched each day, and
a circle for each time the bearded one lay with his
young bride . . . under the blanket . . . he awak-
ened . . . the wall was scratched with circles, many
circles and lines.

Would she call him again? Ever?
When the summons came, he lost count of the
number of steps.
He sat in the same chair, under the same light. This
time, the light was swinging back and forth. The
swing shortened. It stopped.
She came around the table quickly. Nothing in
either hand. Stopped three feet from him. Unbut-
toned her tight tunic. With both hands, in one swift
movement, she pulled up her blouse. Immense
breasts stared at him. Pink nipples surrounded by
black hair. "You'll never see the breasts of a woman
again. I'll hide you away—in a smaller cell—a far off

place—until you are an old man—never to see the breasts of a woman again."

He forced himself to sit upright. Waited for the blow that never came. He would not speak.

She pulled down her blouse, walked to the door at the left and without turning—*Go*.

Then while he could still reach the bars, he could no longer pull himself up to search the hole for the garlic.

The guard brought the soup to his cell and filled his bowl. It smelled worse than it had ever smelled before. The soup was poisoned. *Do not eat it*. He put it in a far corner of his cell. Later that evening, he arose from his blanket and pissed into the bowl. He tried to sleep. Heard scratchings, squeaking in the dark. A sliver of moon through the courtyard window. Then darkness and sleep.

In the morning, he found the tiniest of mice drowned in the soup-piss, white belly up and front legs curled in prayer.

The mouse had eaten his fill and couldn't climb up the smooth sides.

Or the mouse had been poisoned.

Now he sang the song of the days. Monday to Friday set to an aria of *Othello*. The Moor confessed his love for Desdemona. Monday, Tuesday, Wednesday and so on, the song trilled on.

Then he sang *Ponedel'nik, Vtornik, Sreda, Chetverg, Piatnitza, Subbota, Voskresene's*. When he finished this song, he realized he'd sung the days of the week in Russian, not Yiddish the mother tongue, or Polish that he thought of as the father tongue, but Russian.

It's logical; he's not losing his mind: the days of the week belong to them, to the Russians.

And then his dreams of love disappeared . . . he tried to bring them back . . . instead, he heard the girls of the song . . . *was it Sonya* . . . *was it Tanya* . . . *was it Manya* . . . just the same . . . never slept with these girls . . . they stayed for a while . . . the lady commissar's song . . . and then they all disappeared.

And one day, the jailer comes: I am free.

FOUR

On shaky legs, I walk away from my prison. The sun strikes my head like the wrath of God.

A jacket flaps across my right shoulder. And a cap falls to the ground. I turn and see a blue uniformed back walking in the direction of the prison. I stand there, trying to remember one kindness from any jailer during the nine months.

On with the cap, protection against the scorching sun, and with the jacket over one arm, I walk toward the bazaar. I pull the cap down over my face. The vendors are beginning to close, throwing cloths over the goods, to get ready for their nap in the midday heat.

Two veterans in army castoffs walk abreast; one on crutches, leg in a cast; the other limping and walking with a cane. One grabs a fish; the other takes an apple from under a covered stall. They stop, a bottle appears; they pass it back and forth, stagger on.

A legless veteran on a low cart, pushing himself with a stick in each hand, stops near them. He tugs on the cane of one of the drinkers. This man passes the bottle down to the trunk sitting on the cart. The two drunks laugh, curse, support one another, arms around shoulders.

The half-a-man drinks again, then heaves the bottle high in the air and it flies over the row of stalls and drops into the next row. He speeds away, thrusting with both poles. Stops before a watermelon stand. Grabs a melon and puts it over his tied-back empty pants legs. Poles again. The cart swings sideways, jams. The Kazakh vendor bends over and takes back the melon. The legless one backhands with his pole, striking it against the Kazakh's knee and he falls to the ground with a cry of pain. The melon rolls away. The legless man rides off with powerful thrusts of his two poles.

Now a fourth man, medals dangling from his sergeant's blouse, approaches the two drunkards. From where I stand, behind the strings of fish, I can hear shouts, curses, whore of your mother; but I can't be seen. The veteran drops his cane and smashes the newcomer on the chin with his right fist. The man staggers back. A crutch lashes out across the back of his legs. He falls. He gets up. I see now, the sergeant has two good legs but only half an arm, wrist and fingers missing. With this crippled arm, he grabs the assailant around the neck, pulls him close and hits him again and again with his good fist. He releases his strangle hold and the man slides to the ground. Half-an-arm kicks him with his heavy boots.

I slip away, cross past three rows of stalls and turn in, toward the last few open stalls. "Little mother," I say to a wrinkled Russian vendor, "can you spare a melon? The rottenest one, one you can't sell."

"At least you ask," she says, and reaches under her stand with her foot and rolls a melon toward me.

I snatch it up, break it open and sink my teeth into it. The cool, sweet juice. Scrape, gnaw with my teeth down to the skin.

Now I sidle next to a fish seller who is covering his dried fish with a cloth. "Your oldest fish," I tell him, "to me would make a feast."

He looks at me scornfully. "A Jewish beggar, and a young man too. Here," and he throws a fish at me, "get out of my sight." I catch the fish against my chest, put it into my jacket pocket. The fish is so hard, I could easily break Tibor's skull with it.

"Thank you, little father."

"Don't little father me. Those hooligans. I'm packing up." He takes two baskets from under his clothesline of wires and starts tearing off fish and throwing them into the baskets.

I start yanking fish off. With each pull—I yank Tibor by his beard: he wormed the story from my sister; he gave away my hiding place; betrayed me to the militia. "Why don't the police stop them?"

"No one stops them. They push to the front of lines. Take what they want. Afraid of no one. Even the four-letter men turn their heads aside. The more medals they wear, the worse they are."

"It's hard on you honest merchants."

He covers one basket with a cloth. "The young people are ruined. Just the other day . . . ah, never mind. Where have you been that you find this so strange? Just give me that other basket now, and move on."

"Where can I find work, any work?"

"A comedian too. Give me that basket."

"Where are you from? Poland?"

"Never mind where I'm from. Hand over that basket."

I lift it and he snatches it from me.

"You really want work? Try the station. You can always earn a few roubles as a porter." He turns away and over his shoulder calls, "Young fellow, watch out for the porters' union."

I walk through the thinning crowd, slip behind a stall once, when I think I see Tibor, the thief-husband, dirtier than ever, walking arm in arm with Dov, the King of the Thieves. I'll have to wait. I search for a rock, find a fist-sized one and drop it into my coat pocket. It falls through the lining, so I transfer it into the pocket with the fish. I set out for Genia's house. I can wait, until darkness and he returns home alone.

A cry in back of me, "A circus, a circus," and people rouse themselves from their resting places in the shade of the houses, doors are thrown open, and

I let myself go with the flow of the crowd toward the railway station.

The engine whistles, cars are coupled and uncoupled, mail unloaded. On the platform, I count thirty, forty midgets. Mothers and fathers stroll arm in arm. A midget grandfather, silk top hat, white vest and tails, two children hanging on to his coat.

We wait for the clowns, the strongman, horses and bears, there are always bears, to come out from the green baggage cars. More midgets disembark, dressed like ordinary people; one strokes his beard and twirls a watch chain. Two young women put up parasols and walk up and down. Fat midgets with stuffed short arms and legs, big heads. And a romantic pair, two perfectly formed miniatures—a boy and girl, arms linked, ignoring everyone, stroll with the others.

From another car, eight shaven heads, full size men in rags, hands on their heads come out surrounded by militia. They are lined up by twos and with a few shoves, are marched off.

The crowd grows silent. We wait for the act to begin. The engine whistles and at this signal, the little people start for the car steps. Three small men form a human chain and help drag the others up the steps. One by one. Then we watch as they take their seats and it is only then, as the train starts that they acknowledge us—the audience—and they wave and blow kisses through the windows as the train pulls out of the station.

The train travels northward. What will they do, these little ones, in the forests of Siberia?

Now to work. I put on my jacket, keep the hands

free and begin to weave through the refugees still on the platform. A stout woman in a kerchief stands surrounded by many bundles. I pick two up, "Come, Bubba, let me help you find a place."

"Thief, thief," she screams, "give me back." I step back as she reaches for me, drop the bundles and hurry off.

I see two arriveniks, a slight man in a skullcap and his gaunt wife who is wearing three dresses, one on top of the other and a city hat. "Let me help," I say in Yiddish, and pick up a suitcase tied with rope and two hatboxes. "You wife reminds me of an actress I once knew."

"A singer, she is," the man says. "Tatyana Gruzin, you've heard of her?"

"Yes, sure, now come along. You need a bath, a place to stay, food."

They follow me to the Turkish baths and I tell them to go inside and ask the lady who sells tickets where to find a room. Ten roubles tip!

That is all for the day. But the next few days, I manage better. I wait for each train's arrival. Catch the new ones as they come out, pushed from the train doors like cannon balls from a cannon. Dazed. Lost. Into my arms. I collect kopecks, roubles, a cap, a pair of worn leather slippers that I exchange for my own, and trade for food at the bazaar. The weather stays warm, no rain, and after the cemetery and the cell sleeping out of doors in an alley next to a building suits me fine.

The fifth day, I help a Pole from Semipalatinsk. He's spent two years in Siberia and heard it's better here.

He tells me about the ink soul in charge of his camp, worse than my Commander. He claims he knew my father, mother—a liar. I offer him a piece of bread and a bit of goat's cheese. He takes a bottle of vodka from his pack and I take two good drinks. He finishes the bottle and I have to help him sit down between his two packs. He is nodding, hands around both of his bundles. He's forgotten to pay me. Surely he meant to give me a few roubles. So I reach into his pack—his eyes are closed, lip-burbling horse sounds, snores— and I pull out a fine embroidered shirt. Soon they'll come and pick him clean. I loosen my belt, stuff the shirt into my waistband and return to the station.

A herd of nomads, Uzbeks, arrive with the next train. A few windows are thrown open, and they jump to the station platform. I search for Europeans, for the sheep to be shorn, when two hard-faced porters, ignoring trade, begin to push their way toward me. One eye on them, I start to back off. Cossacks! Or worse, Ukrainians, and only fifty feet away. I turn to run and from nowhere receive a clout on the shoulder that spins me half-way round. A fist drives into my back; I grab a Kazakh around the neck. Must not fall. The boots can kill. I hang on to the Kazakh, use him as a shield, look over his shoulder. A stout porter with doubled up fists is waiting for his comrades. Reach into my pocket, grab the stone, slip under the Kazakh's armpit, and smash the porter across the temple. He crumples to the ground. I tramp on his outstretched hand, step over him, hear shouts, and rock in hand, I'm running at full speed, slow down when I pass two militia, then at a trot around the station house, and with each step I fly higher, the rabbit bites the fox, the rabbit bites the fox, out of town and I don't stop until I reach the cemetery, and on hands and knees, I creep through the low brush until I'm well hidden from the road. I cannot stay here, the place of my betrayal, so after it gets dark, I sneak back to Ili and curl up against the wall of the bathhouse and try to sleep.

The shirt brings five hundred roubles. For two hundred roubles I buy a knife from a Kazakh, his own, made from a cut-down scythe and honed to a razor's edge on two sides. He throws in the cowhide sheath. Now I make quick trips to the station, one eye out for the porters; the hell with customers, and look for a way out of accursed Ili. Another place, anywhere I am unknown, Dzhambul, Tashkent, or even Samarkand. The road or the train? The road, too slow and I must carry food, water or hitch a ride on a truck. Too risky.

I see her, the same gold teeth. She's dressed up today. Navy uniform, hammer and sickle on the collar, skirt, cap. She is talking to a railroad official. I wait, buffetted by the crowd moving toward the train to Alma Ata. Another man comes up to her, his hand crosses hers, her hand reaches into her treasure house, between her breasts and comes up empty. She is renting her stateroom.

I push my way through. "Dearest Conductora, my benefactor. . . ."

She draws herself up, pulls in her stomach, raises her chest, a blank stare. Then while I look around and back to her, try to catch her eyes, a faint smile. "The train is full."

"It was full last time."

"So, you are such a fine gentleman, you always travel first class?"

"First class? Yes, you are a first class woman, never have I met someone among my own kind," the whistle drowns my words, so I raise my voice, "with such kindness and hospitality unknown. . . ."

"Stop! You wear me out. Go around to the back, the track side, a few open doors, get on and if the militia don't catch you and if. . . . Go!" She pushes me in the chest and I'm off.

The train is packed like a herring barrel. And smells like one. I don't try for a seat in a compartment; look for a good place in the aisle. After a while, it is impossible to move so I just sit in place, flanked by an Uzbek family on my left and a fat gypsy woman to my right. They ask no questions. The knife sheath punches into my groin so I shift it around to my back. I still have my stone, fondle it in my hand; the stone swells, pulses, grows smoother, beats; the gypsy's back is sweat stained, no waist to her; she cradles her head on her pack.

I doze, awaken, and the conductress passes by and goes into the nearest compartment. I close my eyes again. A baby's wailing and I sit up and the gypsy woman is nursing a black-haired child at one huge breast. The child gasps, hiccups and the gypsy gives her the other tit. A smell of diarrhea. The gypsy turns to me and in good Polish, "If only I had some water, I could wipe her off, clean her."

I stay mute.

The baby screams, a high-pitched sound. "I'm meeting my husband and family in Chymkent. We were separated. If only. . . ."

The train is pulling into Alma Ata.

My father told me about the Endecks who beat up Jews and gypsies alike. Is he alive, my father? Who is caring for him? Marian is too selfish and Genia with child and fifty kilometers distant. Never volunteer, never step forward, the old-timer said in Siberia. "I'll get you water."

She hands me a pot from her pack. I push my way off, get on a long line at the water spout. It moves slowly. I'll never make the train with this cursed pot. Shift from foot to foot. Then I step out of line, make a dash for the barber shop. Inside, I look around—new faces—run up to the head barber, my old boss, "It's Mendel, Max, you remember me? I must have water."

"You're back and without a mark on you. I could use a good barber."

"Water, please *tovarisch*. I'll tell you all later. Water."

He points to the pail nearby and I fill my pot, hear the train whistle, back to the platform, and fight my way aboard.

Ah, the look she gave me when I set the pot before her.

When the train nears Dzhambul, the compartment doors open and the travelers carrying bundles flood into the corridor. I get up to keep from being trampled upon and stand over the gypsy woman and her baby, hands against the wall, body arched over them. She grasps my belt and pulls herself to her feet. She grabs my neck in a stranglehold and kisses my forehead, my nose, cheeks. I pull away and enter the nearest empty compartment. Tug at a window. Push against it, hammer the bottom with my fist. Still can't open it. I take out my knife, pry around the window edges, lever the knife carefully, then as the train slows, I pull again. The window opens and I sit on the edge, turn, hang down and drop to the tracks.

I let the train pull ahead and follow the tracks to the station. A small settlement of clay houses lies on one side of the platform; then the road to Dzhambul winds seven or eight kilometers into town.

Four ragged men are carrying a coffin. Barefoot Uzbek children surround them, some throw stones and shout, "Hallo-hallo, dead ones." That's what they call the Polish Jews. The Russians are called swine while they shout *Ishak*, donkey, at the Uzbeks. I have seen Uzbek mothers scream in fear at pigs loose in the streets and gather their children around them. If no Russian appears to reclaim the lost pig, an Uzbek will draw his knife from his boot, kill the pig and drag the carcass away from his home. Leave it to rot and stink.

One hundred feet from the station, a girl swings from a bar fastened to a tree branch by two thick ropes. A flash of red tights. Two carts and a larger wagon are drawn up around a nearby yurt and three donkeys are tethered to a smaller tree. I push my way through the onlookers as two doves fly off the girl's shoulders and circle overhead; necks are craned and the doves return to their resting place. The fat girl swings gently, barely four feet off the ground; she beats her legs, her white petticoat flies up—a plump red V exposed. She smiles, waves one hand at the crowd and blows fat kisses.

Near her stands a middle-aged man, long black

hair and heavy beard, frock coat, hatless. He holds a whip curled in one hand.

A burly Kazakh comes out of the yurt, bare to the waist, in white baggy trousers. He leads a brown bear on a chain. Those nearest the bear pull back as I push my way to the front. The bear's white-flecked muzzle is covered with a heavy leather cage. A Russian elbows me. "You Jews have a rotten habit, always first in line even for typhus."

"Comrade, comrade," I say to him. "You want to fight? Fight your friend over there—the bear."

The ringmaster points his whip at the swinging girl. The bear, now on hind legs, swats the air with his paws like a boxer. "Our circus has performed before the highest officials in Moscow. We have just come from a performance before thousands under the gates of the Emir's palace in Bukhara." His voice changes. "The villainous Emir! How many of your forefathers were beheaded by his scimitars until he was laid low by Soviet power, no longer able to tyrannize over the good farmers and proletariat of your beautiful land. Praise be to Allah."

The bear growls softly, whimpers and scratches the back of his neck. "Throughout all Uzbekistan, crowds gather to see our trapeze artist, our dancing bear who wrestles all comers, our all-powerful Kazakh wrestler, Konal, and many other wonders. In a little while, you can test your best quail against our Mahmoud," and he points to an Old Uzbek, turbaned, a wisp of a white beard, who fondles a quail in one fist, petting the brown bird, transferring it from hand to hand.

The ringmaster points his whip at the smiling girl and she slides off the bar. The Kazakh puts his free hand under her behind and raises her high in the air. The bear rushes at the Kazakh who hold the animal off with his other hand against the bear's caged face. The bear sits and crosses his arms over his chest. The Kazakh sets the smiling girl on the ground. She drapes one arm around the bear's neck. The bear sticks out his rough, black tongue. Ringmaster, Kazakh, red-tights lady and bear stand abreast, raise their right fists, chorus, "Long live Comrade Stalin and victory to the glorious Red Army."

The bear will be picked up soon as an enemy of the Soviet, I am sure; he didn't say a word, just started scratching furiously again.

The crowd opens in back of me and as I turn around, six NKVD men, pistols behind and smoke pouring from their faces, cut through the onlookers. Their leader throws his cigarette on the ground, stamps on it and faces the ringmaster. The Kazakh hastily pulls the bear back to the yurt and with kicks and shoves, forces him inside. I slip over to a cart and lean against it, currying a donkey with my fingers. I can't hear but see the ringmaster produce papers, beat the air with his fist. The girl brings a bottle of vodka; it's passed around and the NKVD men stroll away.

Quickly now, the yurt is dissambled and packed in the large wagon. The trapeze is removed from the tree. Closed boxes, a *mangalka*, the Uzbek bottomless pail, lined with clay, three boxes overflowing with clothing-costumes, a sack of dried prunes, a few fall out and the Kazakh pops them into his mouth, other sacks, everything is packed onto the large wagon and one two-wheeled cart; the donkeys are hitched up;

the bear is urged into a four-wheeled cart; the ringmaster and girl get into the lead wagon, "Out of our way," he says to me.

"I want to join your circus, Comrade Ringmaster," I say, looking up at him.

"What can you do?"

"I'm a barber but I know horses, animals, can care for them, do anything."

"I need a juggler. Can you juggle six razors?"

"I can learn."

Like a magician, he brings out six red balls and one after the other, he throws them at me. I catch two, the others roll away, and start to juggle with one hand. Instant success. I'm a barber-juggler.

"Out of the way. Pick up those balls and hand them over."

I pick up one and try three balls in two hands. Drop them.

The girl climbs down from the cart and picks up three balls, oh how she bends, and I hand her two balls. She cradles the five against her bosom with one hand. I step between the girl and the wagon, shielding us with my back, give her the last ball with my left and caress the back of her hand with my right.

The ringmaster drops the reins, stares over my head, looks down the road. "Are you a clown? A trick rider?"

"Golubchek," the girl says. "Stop it. We have no horses."

"Yes," he answers dreamily, "we had a horse. A white horse and five others, too, and three clowns and a high wire act, a lion. . . ."

"Golubchek, that old lion. If Juhk, our dear bear,

hadn't broken the lion's ribs, the cat would have died of starvation in a week. And . . ."

"We had a leopard and six monkeys and two bears on bicycles. . . ."

"You sold them, Igor, remember?"

"You remember those two other tricksters, Ursula, don't you? Remember when Juhk was a young, strong bear, the best hockey playing bear in Moscow."

"I never knew him then, little father. He's older than I am."

"Come, blessing of my old age. Don't stand near that scarecrow. There are a thousand barbers or whatever he is like him in Dzhambul. Come!"

He gives her a hand up, into the wagon. She reaches into a sack behind her and as Golubchek urges the donkey on with a slap of the reins, she holds one fist out. I cup my hands under it and a stream of raisins dribbles out. I stuff my mouth with the tasty fruit and watch the caravan roll down the road to Dzhambul.

I follow the last cart, a two wheeler, with an Uzbek driving. The middle cart holds the bear, a tarpaulin thrown over him.

I pick up two round stones from the roadside and start to juggle. When the road turns, the girl looks back. It's easy to keep up with them. Golubchek is on and off the wagon seat, going from the second to third cart and back again. Soon I gather a third stone and I stop to concentrate on the juggling. In a little while, I am a three-stone juggler. A gray body lies three feet from the road. I could use a pair of boots, but boots, shirt, pants have been stripped. Farther on, two men are digging a long trench in the field. Nearby stands a large wagon covered with a tarpaulin. A bare leg sticks out from under the tarp, hangs over the wagon's edge.

A group of Jews in torn, wadded jackets pass by on the way to the station. The circus caravan is out of sight. I cut across a field; the black-faced sheep scatter; bearing right, I stay in the field, skirting sheep droppings and farther on, I rejoin the road. Stand there, juggling three stones.

In a little while, Golubchek and the girl, riding behind the lead donkey, come into sight. I continue juggling. As they come abreast, I throw the stones higher and higher.

The lead wagon halts. Golubchek gets out and goes to the side of the road to relieve himself. The girl goes to the other side and squats behind some bushes. I drop my stones and join Golubchek, dangle with him. "Your Jews are the finest people in the whole universe," he says shaking his cock, "too good for this world, so Hitler is helping them on their way to a better place. Go away! Don't bring your trouble on us."

I've seen that he is circumsized and, whatever he is, he's not a Moslem.

The caravan rides on. The girl waves a tiny wave. Golubchek takes his knife from his boot and wipes it on his pants leg, replaces it.

Now they have stopped, drawn the wagons in a circle, and the Uzbek and Konal are gathering branches for a fire. Golubchek lights the fire inside the *mangalka* and the girl places two pots above the flames. I wait, out of earshot. The bear feeds from a large washbasin. It looks like millet or another grain. The others scoop food from the smaller pot with pieces of bread. My feet hurt in my thin, leather slippers. I need a pair of boots. Food! I pick up another stone and become a four-stone juggler.

Konal rises from the fire and walks toward me. I open my coat so he can see my knife. His bald head glistens, sweat runs down his neck across his bare chest. I'd rather fight the bear. Run again or stay?

Konal stops ten feet away. "Peace be with you, juggler with a knife, a Kazakh blade." He thrusts out his hand. "The girl sent this." I step forward two steps, hesitate. "Take it. Pilaff."

I take the thick slices of black bread, raise it up, lick the fat-soaked rice dripping out. Tongue the bread all around the edges. "Why are there so many dead ones along the roadside?"

"Typhus. It was worse in Chymkent, worse yet in Samarkand. If you catch this plague, you may die or you may recover and live one hundred years."

"Thank the girl for me. She saved my life." I want him to go, go, so I can devour the tasty bread and rice. "I will join you soon."

"Not yet. Igor says he can only use a six-ball juggler."

"Igor?"

"Igor Golubchek, our leader, once the finest wrestler in all Georgia. Although I outweigh him by twenty kilos, and I'm younger by twenty years, he can still give me a tussle."

"You have two wrestlers! Must I become a wrestler too?"

"Only a six-ball juggler," he turns away and calls back, "but I will tell him you carry a sharp knife."

I try to eat slowly, savor the rice and carrots, even a bit of meat inside. A stringy piece of meat catches in my teeth. I chase my tongue after it, dislodge and swallow it. Thirsty now, but the only water lies in a roadside puddle. I see a tree that looks like it bears *tutovniks*, the sweet, pale yellow berries. No luck, the bottom branches that I can reach have already been stripped. So I draw closer to the caravan and settle down thirty feet away, legs crossed.

The girl pours tea into metal mugs. The bear gets up from the shade of a cart and squeezes between Golubchek and the girl. The bear pushes Golubchek with his rump. He is unmuzzled. Golubchek raises one fist above his head. A low warning growl; the bear chomps his jaws and clicks its teeth together. The girl gives Golubchek a playful shove and he backs away on hands and heels, sits ten feet off. The bear sits on his rump and twirls a fist in the air. The girl throws her arm around his neck, sticks out her tongue at Golubchek.

"Hey, Juggler. Come here!"

I walk toward Golubchek who pats the ground near him. I sit. The girl brings tea and drops a spoonful of apricot preserves into it. I hold the cup in two hands, sip slowly.

"There are thieves everywhere," he says. I nod. "I need a man to watch our carts and goods when we go to the bazaar to trade. You have a knife. Can you use it?"

"I'm your man. I can juggle four balls."

"Enough with the juggling! Six, eight, ten balls.

Who cares! Konal," he shouts. "Bring me one of those clubs."

Konal takes a stout three-foot club from a cart. He tosses it high in the air. Golubchek somersaults backwards, lands on his feet and catches it with a flourish. "Another one," he shouts. Konal throws another club up, it turns end over end and Golubchek grabs it. "Another." He catches the third and then clubs fly up in the air, down, are caught again, rise, one club hits another, sends it up, "Another," and Konal takes a fourth club, walks closer and more carefully, he wafts this one into the air. Now clubs fly high and turning, behind Golubchek's back and turning, spinning; he speaks as the clubs rise and fall, "It's not fitting . . . for a ringmaster . . . to play the juggler . . . sometimes I wish I could perform again . . . alone . . . before thousands . . . not be responsible for . . . bang, bang, bang, bang, he fires the clubs one after the other at the side of the nearest cart. Hits the same spot.

The bear rises on its hind legs, snorts and makes a whistling, whoosh, whoosh sound.

He turns to me. "You can break a man's skull if you learn to throw it right. Now pick one for yourself and throw the others back into the cart." I get up and he claps me on one shoulder, "Juggler, you are in my circus."

"Mahmoud," he calls to the Uzbek, "these are your people. See if the farmer will let us stay here for a few nights."

The Uzbek gets up and adjusts his turban, pulls his coat around him. He waits.

Golubchek pulls a rough shirt from a box and

hands it to the Uzbek. "Give him this gift and when you leave him, if you must, this bag of raisins." Mahmoud ties the bag to his belt, under his wadded coat, and heads across the field toward the *kibitka*.

Then with the single word, "Watch," to me, he kisses the girl, beckons Konal, and the two of them head for town.

I am alone with her. She outweighs me by twenty kilos.

The girl muzzles the bear, chain to his collar, and shoos him into the cart. He settles down with a satisfied grunt. Ursula fastens his chain to a hook on the floor of the cart. "Come," she says, "we can sit there in Mahmoud's cart. He will be awhile if I know him."

She hoists herself into the back of the cart and I join her.

"Your father loves you very much."

"He is not my father."

"Your uncle?"

"He claims he bought me from the gypsies in Poland. When I was a year old."

"You're very fair, such pretty skin, not at all like a gypsy."

"Sometimes he says he took me from an orphanage in Lodz."

"Is that true?"

"Whatever comes to his mind, he says. I have been everywhere with Igor. Once we traveled in style, our own railroad car form Moscow to Kharkov to Rostov to Tiflis, many places; then the war. No food for humans; how could we keep the animals alive? The midgets ran away first. They heard the Germans kill

Jews, gypsies, midgets. Now we are all that's left. Four of us, and one old bear."

"Five."

"Yes, with you, five."

The sun is beginning to set and a slight breeze rises from the southeast. She reaches for a blanket behind her. "Put this around you. You need a warmer coat for the night." She drapes half the blanket around her heavy shoulders.

"So your guardian is a Pole?"

"Who knows? Some days he admits to being a Pole. Then he claims he is from Tiflis, a Georgian, and that is where he learned to wrestle as a young man. Once he told me he was descended from the Kantonists. You know who they are?"

I shake my head, draw closer under the blanket.

"Years ago, the story goes, a hundred years or more, Jewish orphans were taken into the Russian Army at the age of seven or eight. The army raised them and at conscription age, they become soldiers and served the Czar for twenty-five years. Igor says his grandfather was a Kantonist and had a high position in Imperial Russia. Igor had a Jewish wife and child too. She ran away; she didn't like circus life."

"You know a lot." She asks nothing about me.

"I know nothing. Will you teach me to read and write Yiddish? I can write my name in Yiddish—Anna. That's all."

"He calls you Ursula."

"That means she-bear in a foreign tongue. I'm Anna. He lets no one near me."

"Although I am not learned, I'll teach you to read. We'll need pencils, paper, books."

"There are none."

"Then tomorrow, we'll trace letters in the sand. Aren't you afraid, alone here while you wait for them to return? I mean before I joined you. With me," and I touch my dagger hilt, "you do not have to be afraid."

Mahmoud has returned. I see his cigarette glowing in the darkness.

"Now stand here," she says, "at the cart's edge, and put your hand here." She positions my hand, elbow on the cart end. "I'll put my hand here." She puts her elbow next to mine, grasps my palm. "Now put my hand down."

"Why? I like to hold your palm, touch the softness of it." I draw closer, rest my leg alongside her thigh. Smell her, a clean smell like a fresh *lyepushka* with butter.

She draws back. "Let's see how strong you are." She begins a steady pressure on my palm, forces my arm back.

I resist, push back, until we are locked, both arms upright. I exert more force. Can't budge her. With an easy, irresistible pressure, she forces my hand down to the cart bed.

"You're too thin, Juggler. Now you'll take out your knife; Force me. Go ahead, Juggler, you see I am not afraid of thieves."

"I'll never force you." I take the blanket from the cart and start toward Konal's cart. The bear sleeps there! So I turn about and push the donkeys aside and bed down near them. Roll up in the blanket. The Uzbek smokes on. My fate: always with freaks. A

Polish cook old enough to be my mother; a tramp in Ili, who wants rolls, always rolls, and Turkish baths; a Russian conductora with a boyfriend in every station, dirty, black with coal dust from fucking with the stoker; and now a fat girl who sleeps with a bear.

She calls out. "Tomorrow you'll teach me to read. You promised."

After breakfast of boiled millet and tea, Golubchek loads a sack each for Konal and Mahmoud and they are off for the bazaar. Inside, they have stuffed icons, wooden buttons, prunes, raisins, underwear, and caps. They return each evening with food and once with three sacks of millet to feed the bear.

When the men leave, our lessons begin, and soon Anna knows the entire Yiddish alphabet. She wants words then, and I draw simple words in the sand. The bear sleeps tied to the wagon and when he awakens he looks at me menacingly. Once I chase off three beggars by just picking up my stick and rapping the sides of a cart. They curse in foul Yiddish, cursing my mother, grandfather, all the way back to Abraham and Isaac. I carry water from the Uzbek farmer's irrigation ditch. Anna washes. I doze, open my eyes and her strong arms are rubbing and twisting clothing in the bear's pan.

At night, when we sit around the fire, and take our portions of food, good food, herring and tomatoes and carrots and good black bread or lamb and rice and carrots in a savory stew, Anna takes her share and divides it in half and gives half to me. I have never eaten so well. Not since Zamoscz. She grows thinner. Golubchek says he'll have to find a new fat lady. She blushes, I think. A week passes this way.

I ask her when will we give a performance. It's Igor's circus, she answers. Why don't we rehearse, practice. I still juggle four balls, can't make the fifth. We all know our jobs, she says.

A band of Uzbeks comes toward us, late one afternoon. Seven or eight settle down on the dry grass thirty feet away and a young boy approaches, scrawny and lice-bitten, on crude crutches. He holds out two hands for food. Anna opens a sack of millet and fills his tiny cupped hands. He asked for more for his mother at home, for the babies.

The seven are on us! Two push Anna to the ground. The others swarm over the wagon and start to drag out the open sack. I scramble to my feet and strike one across the back with my club; two others leap from the wagon and I swing my club in wide circles, holding them off. They circle and I move with them. Another leaps on my back, bears me to the ground. He reaches for my knife. I twist over onto my back, grab his wrist with one hand, knee him in the groin. A bare foot pins my left wrist to the ground.

I hear the bear snarling, chain rattling. I'm free. They scatter and run off. Juhk is after them, hauling the cart at the end of his chain. Anna brings him back, still clicking his teeth and chomping his jaws. Little rheumy eyes sparkling. I lay gasping against a cart wheel. My chin is scraped raw. The bear paces on all fours, back and forth, rises on hind legs, swings his arms in his boxing routine, then finally lies down.

Anna croons to him, pets his head, runs her hand alongside his neck, massages him.

Finally, she comes to me. On her knees, she washes my face with a wet cloth; her full breasts against me like two fresh loaves of white bread; I look between them, down, down, deep into the cleft. I pull her to me—a kiss—apricot jam—dizzy—the bear rattles its chain, bear and cart start to move and Ursula-Anna pushes against my chest with both hands and gets up. *To go to her bear!*

My left wrist throbs and is beginning to swell. I hold the sack open and Anna scoops up millet and sand and pours it back into the sack. She takes a heavy needle and thread and starts sewing a tear in the sack. The sun has disappeared. A pink light in the sky when the men, sacks on their shoulders, come into camp.

"Did they get anything?" Golubchek asks me.

"No."

"Why didn't you use your knife?"

I don't answer.

"And you, Ursula, you've tied the bear to the cart. Why?"

She continues sewing.

"You know he must be tied to the wagon, with the brake on. He could have pulled that cart all the way to Afghanistan."

"How many?" Konal says.

"Seven or eight. Maybe nine. Uzbeks." I don't tell them, two may have been Jews.

"You've done well," Konal says. "Here, some *Makhorka*." He hands me the tobacco wrapped in a sheet of newspaper. "And matches." He takes the bear's chain, undoes it from the cart, leads him to the wagon and reties him.

Golubchek grasps my shoulder, shakes me, "Come." He extends his hand and I clasp it with my right, the uninjured one and he hoists me to my feet. I follow him to the wagon. He climbs in, lifts a floorboard, pulls back a cloth. A large black pistol lies there. "If you need it, next time, it's loaded and ready."

"How do I get it with the bear tied alongside?"

"You'll find a way," and he rewraps the pistol lovingly, replaces the board, and puts a sack over it. Then he takes a key from his belt, opens a lock on a large wooden chest and throws back the cover. "Look!" He raises a blue-spangled dress, fondles it, then drags out two clown costumes, a black suit, a red dress. He looks at me.

"Beautiful, beautiful." I know what he expects.

He holds up a clown suit next to me, shakes his head sorrowfully. "You'll need boots. I have no boots." Then he throws everything back, jumps on the box, does a little jig, throws his arms about, down from the box, springs up again, dancing away and he vaults to the ground with one leap, squats, legs go out, back, up, down, long hair flying. Abruptly, he stops. He's not at all winded. "We are the finest circus in all Uzbekistan! Let's drink to that!" He takes a bottle from the wagon, passes it to me. Ah, how the good vodka burns everything away. A thin rain begins to fall. We grab our blankets and bed under the wagon and carts. Anna lies between Golubchek and the bear.

The next morning, Golubchek gives me some

handbills and tells me to give them out in the bazaar
and post them anywhere that I can in Dzhambul.
Stay away from the post office and NKVD headquar-
ters. As if I needed this warning.

As I start to leave, handbills under one arm, he
says, "And take Mahmoud, an Uzbek will be handy."

"Am I a prisoner, Igor? A child who needs a
guide?"

"Why are you angry, Max?" The first time he's
called me anything but Juggler. "Mahmoud can help,
you'll finish sooner."

"I need no help!"

"Mahmoud, Golubchek calls, "take these handbills
and go back to the station."

Konal says, "Wait for me, little brother." He pulls a
shirt over his head. "I'll go with you. I must see an
old uncle in Dzhambul. A townsman now, he's left
our hills and valleys for the city life."

I look at the topmost handbill. In Russian and
Uzbek or Kazakh. I can't read their language al-
though I speak Kazakh haltingly. It announces: "The
Great Moscow Circus, Aerial Acts, Jugglers, Five
Hundred Roubles for any Man who Can Stay Three
Minutes in a Ring with Juhk the Bear."

As I walk away, I hear, "Come back safely, Max,"
from Anna.

We soon leave the camp behind. "It is an honor to
walk under the protection of a warrior like yourself,"
Konal says.

"I am honored, Konal, to walk beside the greatest
wrestler in all Kazakhstan."

We walk in silence and soon reach row upon row of
clay huts at the beginning of town. Dirt streets, long

lots stretch back of each house, with orchards and garden plots in each backyard. An ancient place, none of the new concrete buildings like Alma Ata or the busy street cars and honking official cars and trucks. The streets are filled with "runners from the other side." A Jew from Bukhara said that to me once. A poor but proud people; they have lived in Bukhara for centuries and look down on us "refugees."

I hand a notice here and there, wherever I find a vendor taking his goods to the bazaar. "Do you wrestle the bear?" I ask Konal.

"We try to get some local into the ring. Some young strong fellow. Sometimes we can't find one. So, always at the end, I wrestle with Juhk, the great bear. He respects me. First he falls down; then I fall down. He always wins. No man beats Juhk."

I give an Uzbek, carrying a sack, a handbill. He crumples it and spits at my feet.

"And Golubchek, he too wrestles. . . ." I slip the handbills under my coat as we pass two blue-coated militia.

"A fine man, our Igor, but the bear does not trust him."

The crowd thickens as we get closer to the bazaar. Shall I go in, mingle there—I need boots, a gift for Anna. No money and nothing to trade. I've eaten well with the troupe, but only a few chervontsi notes left, my knife and the clothes on my back.

"I leave you soon, Max. Be careful. The tail of a lion lashes back and forth when it's about to attack, Max, but bears—give no warning."

"What do you mean, Konal? Stop speaking in riddles."

"That pockmarked beggar, Max. It's the third street that I've seen him before us. He watches, sits, does not beg."

A side glance. I see him. A turbaned Uzbek. Like the others.

"Farewell, Max," and Konal swings left at a fast pace.

The beggar jumps to his feet, pulls a pistol from under his rags. "Hands up!" He's barring my way, pistol in my belly. "After the other one!" he shouts, and two other men, pistols drawn, chase after Konal. "You! Hands on head."

The handbills are taken from under my arm by a fourth man and I'm marched off at a fast clip to NKVD headquarters.

Family name? First name? Father's name? Where and when born? Papers? Like pistol shots from the interrogator with small slits for eyes set in a white dumpling face. A stone in my belly. I think this interrogator is a Jew! I hope for another later. I've heard some Jews can be the worst: to show they are not playing favorites with their own kind.

"From me, young man," said *Knadlech*-face, "you have nothing to fear. Expect only kindness and understanding. From you I expect only one thing: the truth."

They take my belt, knife, and money. Nearby, in the bare cement-walled room, they strip the laces from three Jews' shoes and these three are led away, shoes flapping, stumbling to their cells. I'm lucky, my felt slippers have no laces. Holding up my pants with one hand, I follow a plainclothesman along a passageway to a door, and he turns me over to a blue prison guard. I pass rooms with thirty or forty men inside but for me, they have reserved something special. I ask to go to the bathroom and my silent guard takes me down a corridor to the stinking latrine. On the walls, above my head I see, as I dangle before the trough, *Beat the kikes and save Soviet Russia.* Then I'm led back to my single room. I sink down to the dirt floor, the door slams shut, the wolf's eye peephole opens and closes, and my guard is gone.

Now I'm shut away forever. A second offender. They'll add three, nine, who knows how many years to my first sentence. When we do not come back—did they catch Konal—Golubchek and the remnants of his crazy circus will leave, never to return.

Anna will disappear into the desert. Mahmoud leaves them. They're all dying of thirst. Jukh and Igor fight over Anna. They die in a death struggle—a bullet between Juhk's bear eyes; Igor's neck broken.

The door opens. The guard sets down kasha groats and a boiled beet in a metal plate and a mug of water on the floor. Not what I'm used to lately, but better than the prison food in Ili. I'll eat, stay strong. After eating and resting a while, I twist and turn, touch the floor, swing my arms, do the kazatzka like Golubchek; hard to do holding my pants with one hand; legs out and back, up, down, until I fall back exhausted.

Do they know I'm here? Can I get a message out? If only I were with other prisoners, I'd have a chance to get word out.

The next day I wait to be called for interrogation.

Anna has pretty legs . . . to get between them . . . and the palest of blue eyes. She must want me

back. I try to remember when the circus performance
goes on. I find two pebbles and lie on my back,
juggling. Find a third and juggle sitting up.

What will they ask? Are you a deserter? I'll promise
to rejoin the army. Escape. The circus will have dis-
appeared. Where? I repeat Golubchek's mad dance. I
stand up and raise both hands and box the great bear,
Juhk.

Sleep. Eat. Under guard to the latrine. Someone
has smeared a brown substance over the word *kikes*
above the trough.

I go to the bazaar and from a stand, I steal a fat,
pink-cheeked *matroshka*. It's a foot high, shaped like a
large egg, and the little mother wears a bright red
dress and a yellow apron. I break it open at the
middle and one by one, take out six littler *matroshkas*,
each one inside the other. In the next to the largest
one I write a message: Anna dearest, little flower.
Then inside each doll I write other messages . . .
*Come with me . . . Leave your bear . . . I'll be father,
brother . . . Everything to you . . . Wait for me . . .*

When I awaken the next day, my first thought: how
do I smuggle the *matroshka* to Anna? I reach under the
bunk, knock over my metal cup. The *matroshka* is
gone.

I dance the kazatzka.

All day.

No one has ever waited.

They all rush off, disappear.

When the guard leaves the evening soup and
bread, I ask him, "Has anyone from the out-
side . . ."

The door slams.

I walk between rows of stalls, must find another *matroshka*. The vendors, standing before their empty stands, raise their sticks . . . sampling. . . .

I was struck once by a vendor's stick. It's the custom. I sampled an apricot, a few dates, but this merchant smelled a refugee. He struck me across the wrist.

The merchants stand like soldiers: selling air . . . empty stalls . . . finally at one stall, a pock-marked cripple sits cross-legged. A jumble of dirty, eyeless *matroshkas* in his bin. I reach for a doll.

He pulls out a gun, points at my heart. "One hundred roubles."

"I have no money."

"Trade," he says.

"I have nothing."

"Your pants then?"

"No!"

He cocks his pistol. Click! "Pants!"

I take off my pants.

"Shirt. Shoes. Underwear too!"

I stand naked, shivering.

"Jew," he says, "take your stupid doll."

Doll cradled in one arm, I walk back, between the rows of stalls. The merchants strike their stands with their sticks, chanting: "Jew, Hallo-hallo, Jew."

After stale bread and tea, the door swings open again. The guard beckons and I follow him down the corridor. Pass two prisoners sweeping the floor, they don't look up, another carrying a can of slops—into a room. I look for the fat-faced interrogator. A square-shouldered woman behind a table calls out, "Max Schmulovicz, come here."

I stand before her, see my belt on the table. "Sign here," she says, "that everything was returned in good order." I don't dare ask for my knife, money—sign quickly, start to turn away.

"What's your job in the circus?" she asks.

"I wrestle the bear."

She smiles, not a bad-looking Russian, maybe one of our kind. "I hope you win."

I'm off, hand holding up my pants.

"Come back! Take your belt, comrade."

Outside, I'm ready to leap and dance. Around a corner and Igor and Anna rush up to me, hug me. Anna smothers me with kisses. She takes my belt, bends over and starts threading it through my pant's loops. She squeezes me around the waist in a bear hug.

"She did it," Igor says. "Little Anna. Now let's go, down to the square. We must get ready."

With Igor and Anna linking my arms, they hurry me along while Anna tells about my rescue. When I did not return, Mahmoud went to town and made inquiries. He found that I had been picked up and held. Anna followed the fat-faced one for three days until she saw him entering a barber shop. She cornered him outside and told him I was essential for the circus preformance. It had been postponed, until my release. She invited the officials and their wives for a special performance in their honor. Gifts for the wives: her red dress, another silk blue print from China, the red, yellow and green fat lady's gown, three bottles of perfume, underwear, tins of hard candy. A prince's ransom! They are coming tonight.

At the edge of the bazaar, the three wagons are drawn up in a U formation with the big wagon in the middle. Barefoot children stand nearby, just out of reach of the sleeping Juhk. Mohmoud hops off a cart, bows to me. "I dreamed of a young mountain goat, leaping from crag to crag. And you are back. It is Allah's will." Then he sits down, lights a cigarette, and talks to his brown quail, whispering in the bird's ear.

"It's time for you to get to know Juhk better, Max," Anna says.

"I know him well enough."

"I mean run your hand through his coat, let him smell you."

"He doesn't look too interested. Look at him. He didn't even get up to say, 'Welcome back, Max. Glad to see you again.'"

"Come," she says, taking my hand and drawing me closer to the bear. Now he opens his eyes, yawns—purple-black gums and yellow teeth. "Sit next to him," she urges. "Pet him. Run your hand along his back. He likes that."

I draw back. Run my hand from her shoulder around to her waist. Keep it there.

The bear gets up. "See," she says, "Juhk's not angry, he likes you."

"Dearest Ursula-Anna, why are you promoting a love affair with Juhk?"

"You're wrestling him tonight, Max."

"What did you say?"

"You're wrestling Juhk. We promised."

"I won't do it. Find Konal." I look toward Igor who is helping Mahmoud set up a plank on two barrels.

They are searching for a piece of even ground. "Igor,"
I call out to him. "I must see you."

He strolls over, wiping his hands on his trousers.

"What's this about wrestling the bear?"

"Max—we promised the NKVD. The four-letter
men expect it, the climax of our show."

I look from Anna whose face bears the softest look
of entreaty to Igor who stands unsmiling to Juhk who
is now sitting on his rump and seems to be listening
to all that is being said. Jukh yawns.

A pebble flies at Juhk and hits him in the chest. He
gets up, raises onto his hind legs and looks around
majestically. Mahmoud runs after the children and
chases them away.

I should have taken wrestling lessons from Konal
when I had the chance. What good would it do now?
"What do I care! Lions, tigers, bears. I'll wrestle them
all!"

Igor shrugs and walks away. Anna kisses me on the
cheek but I don't return the kiss. I've had enough
kisses.

"Come," she takes my hand in an iron grip, "let's
sit near dear Juhk."

Anna walks up to Juhk, me in tow, motions with a
flutter of her fingers and he sits down. Another
movement with two hands and he lies down, out-
stretched. She draws me down next to him. Starts to
run her hand along his back. Takes my hand and now
I'm massaging the great bear. He turns his head,
stares at me. My heart pounds. She withdraws her
hand. "Good, sweet Juhk. You know Max. He loves
Juhk as much as Ursula. Keep petting him, Max."

I keep stroking. If he bites off my hand, the match is off. Anna croons a wordless song. "Keep stroking him, Max," and when one hand gets tired, I switch hands and continue stroking. The bear sniffs at me, muzzle into my stomach. I become bold and run my hand over his great shoulders, onto his neck. Dust rises from his coat. He gets up and shifts into the shade of the wagon. I follow. He swings his great head. I hesitate, then reach out and stroke the top of his head. Still stroking, I turn to Anna. "If only I could get him to sit still, put a cloth around him and give him a shave and a haircut. It would be a great act."

"Never mind that, Max," she laughs. "You're a wrestler now."

In spite of Anna's urging, I can't eat my dinner. No time for cooked food; the dried lamb on bread keeps balling up in my mouth, until I spit it into my hand. "You need your strength, Max," and she forces two handfuls of raisins on me.

The crowd is gathering in front of the plank seat, covered now with a blue cloth; groups of nomads sitting together, a knot of Jews, other Europeans, and a few Russians. All face the large wagon where Igor has fastened a hammer and sickle flag on a tall stick.

Anna leads me behind the wagon and makes me take off my pants and put on white baggy trousers. She holds a long-tailed cotton shirt in her hand. "Off with that shirt, Max, and put this on."

Igor appears. "Why are you covering his chest? Konal wrestled bare-chested. I too."

"Such a chest?" Anna runs her fingers over my

breastbone and across my ribs. "Why should he get scratched?"

"Igor, you know about animals, birds too. Can I ask you a question?"

"Quick, quick."

I pull on the shirt. Anna buttons the right shoulder.

"My father took me on a long journey once, near the sea. A strong wind was blowing. We turned our backs to the wind, ate a sandwich, drank tea. . . ."

Igor looks away from me, around the wagon at Mahmoud, and then looks back. "Wind, tea, what is it?"

"The gulls on shore huddled together, facing into the wind. Into it. Why?"

"With their backs to the wind, their fathers would open up and they'd lose their body heat. Hurry, hurry. Mahmoud and his quail can only entertain them so long." He handsprings, squats, hand-springs, and is gone. His head darts back around the wagon's side. "Come Anna, come—I want you swinging from the bar with the doves. Now! It calms them."

Anna says, "You look fine." She puts both hands on my shoulders, looks into my eyes. On my eye level, a strapping girl. "First, we ask for volunteers to wrestle Juhk. There may be none. So you will go on. Juhk knows what to do. He'll swing his arms fero-ciously. Just duck under and dance around him. Before three minutes are up, he'll push you out of the ring either with a sweep of his hand . . ." I listen, ears straining, "or with a shove of his hip."

"What if he takes it into his head to . . . never mind. . . ."

"He will be muzzled. Just don't strike his nose. He'll feel it even through the muzzle. It enrages him."

"Tell the bear I won't strike his nose if he doesn't hit mine."

"You are not wrestling a brown bear, Max. Call him Juhk. By name. You are wrestling Juhk." Anna, legs flashing in her red tights, struts away and I—I do the lucky dance, the kazatzska. I'm good at it now; I can learn anything—handsprings, the trapeze, juggling six balls, anything.

When I walk around the wagons, facing the audience, Mahmoud sits fondling his quail, a pile of roubles next to him. Another Uzbek opens his fist and a white and brown flecked bird prances out. Mahmoud sets his quail down. The birds shift, hop forward. Mahmoud's quail rises in a short flight and swoops down on the white bird that is just getting off the ground. He drives him off. The younger Uzbek bows to Mahmoud and hands him roubles.

While Anna mounts the swinging bar, a dove on each shoulder, Mahmoud's quail drives off another bird. He looks toward Igor and gathers up his bird, pops it into a tiny cage and hangs the cage from a peg on the wagon. He stands near Juhk, now muzzled and chained to the wagon.

Arms folded across my chest, I stand near Igor. He salutes with his whip as the crowd parts and the NKVD men, two of them and three women, take their seats on the bench. It's *Knadlech*-face and a woman wearing Anna's red dress, another shaven-headed man, a giant and his woman in the fat lady's striped gown. I don't remember these two. The third woman is the one who set me free.

"Igor," I say from the side of my mouth, "there's the fat lady you were looking for—your two hundred kilo lady, recruit her."

"You'd joke on the way to the cemetery, eh Max."

"I've been there already, Igor."

"So?"

"I'm back."

At that moment, Anna's doves circle overhead, one returns, and the other sets down on the fat lady's shoulder.

"If that bird shits on her," Igor whispers, "we're done for." The fat lady smiles, then giggles, Igor sighs, and the bird circles in the air, rests on the woman's other shoulder, more kisses, bird to fat lady, woman to bird, then the dove circles the crowd three times and settles back onto Anna's shoulder.

Anna drops back on the bar, hangs by her legs. The doves perch on her red kneecaps. The two Russians stand up for a good look at her swinging bottom. The doves hop onto Anna's ankles. She swings upright and the doves circle and return to her shoulders. The crowd seems pleased. I had expected more. A real trapeze act. I realize Anna is too big, too strong for wild flight into the sky. Perhaps she'll challenge them to arm wrestling. She blows kisses all around, special ones at the NKVD officials. The fat lady blows kisses back. Kiss, kiss—will it never stop.

Igor approaches and Anna leaps into his arms. He raises her aloft, holding her up around the waist. The bear rises, whooshing sounds, swings his arms, tugs at the chain. Hands on Igor's wrists, Anna wrests herself free. The bear sits down.

Mahmoud throws balls one after the other at Igor and he juggles six red balls. Up and up they go. The crowd stirs restlessly. Igors puts down three balls and does a slow kazatzka, juggling three balls while his legs shoot out and back. Then Mahmoud hands him three knives and the knives fly up, around his back, down. He asks the nomads in the front row for another knife. A Kazakh takes one from his belt. He juggles four, gets another from an Uzbek who draws it from his boot. Five knives flash in the air. One after the other, Igor fires each knife at the wagon and they land in a small circle, quivering. He returns the borrowed knives.

Igor cracks his whip. He dedicates the next event to the glory of the Soviet Union, the unbeatable symbol of the great Soviet Socialist Republic, the courageous and fierce brown bear of the motherland. Then it's all a jumble. Challenge—stay three minutes—the louder Igor shouts . . . I stare at Mahmoud who is running a thick rope around four stakes set in the ground, forming a square ring.

Anna leads Juhk by the chain, whispering in his ear. He rises on his hand legs, jabs the air with heavy swings, roars his challenges, stamps his feet.

No challengers.

Igor waits a while. He recites,

> "We shall fight like stallions!
> We shall dip the string of the yellow bow
> into the red blood
> and we shall draw it until it tears.

Three Kazakhs urge a fourth large tribesman to his feet. He stamps in place, flexes his muscular arms. The bear roars. He sits back among his friends. They turn their backs on him.

Igor speaks. "We have another champion, a famous juggler, and now the foremost lightweight wrestler of Eastern Poland, our glorious ally in the struggle against the fascist brutes. He has beaten the champion of Bulgaria. "He has consented to wrestle the great bear Juhk. The Juggler—here he comes!"

I look around, then stride forward, walking the way I imagine a famous wrestler would walk. I stand at one corner of the ring, waiting for the crowd to laugh.

No laughter. A hush descends. I fold my arms across my chest.

Anna leads Juhk to the ring, removes his collar, slips it over his head and muzzle. Whispers in his ear.

I step over the rope, into the square.

Juhk rises on hind legs and steps over. Flatfooted, he moves toward me, arms at his side. I advance, eyes glued to this muzzle. I smell him. Remember the rules, Juhk.

I stop, arms outstretched. He begins to pound the air, steps forward; I duck, slip aside. Again he moves on me, arms swinging in wide arcs; I slip under and come out behind him. He turns. I skip back, then move in. His big paw brushes my shoulder. I fall. It was not a hard blow. I'm tempted to stay down, roll and roll, out of the ring. His big feet are stamping next to me. Great yellow claws in scabby flesh.

I jump up. His arms embrace me. Breathes into my

face. A stink, like rotting meat. Now he is dancing around, clutching me to him. I hold him tight. We're one. If he tightens his grip. . . . On we whirl, around and around. Everything swims before my eyes. Faces blur. I think I see Anna over Juhk's shoulder, then she disappears. Father, mother, sisters—faces fly toward me and fly away—Konal comes—his mouth forms words—then he's gone. Juhk's arms loosen. I slide to the ground.

Anna slips into his grasp, one hand on Juhk's shoulder. The bear is doing a waltz step, one, two, three, one, two, three. Anna looks into his eyes adoringly. I crawl out of the ring, stub my foot on the rope. I look at the loving couple. When will they stop? On the dance goes. Anna, head thrown back, still smiles—her stage smile? Stop. Stop.

On they dance.

She wants to stop.

Juhk dances on.

She can't stop. Why doesn't Igor stop them?

On the dance goes.

I crawl away. I get up and climb into the wagon. The clothes chest has been rifled. Empty. I push it aside. Lift the loose board. Unwrap the gun. I pick it up, hold it at my side. I'll go close to him, can't fire at this distance. Blow his brains out.

A strong hand grabs my wrist. "Give me that gun," Igor says, "don't be a fool." I tighten my grip on the butt. "Max, listen, they are cheering. The dance is over. Anna and Juhk have done this a hundred times."

I hand Igor the pistol. From the wagon's height, I

can see Juhk and Anna standing side by side, bowing to the crowd. Anna begins to blow kisses once again. Juhk claps his hands over his eyes, his muzzle, and backhands kisses too. Igor says, "Anna will have to teach that bear how to blow a proper kiss."

FIVE

Icollapse onto the clothes chest. Ribs ache every time I take a breath. I rub my right thigh. A shooting pain in the ankle.

The crowd begins to drift away. A black car rolls up and the commissars disappear inside. Two Uzbek children square off and growl and cuff one another while four or five others watch them. Mahmoud takes down the trapeze and flag. Anna urges the bear into the four-wheeled cart.

I get up, slide over the wagon's rear, ease myself to the ground. Test the ankle.

The moon is rising, faint in the sky; sun still up—darkness takes a long while to arrive in this desert land, then the sun can't wait to return, bright and fiery red.

Golubchek, gun still in his waistband, vaults into the head wagon's seat. He wraps the gun in a cloth, opens the chest. I see now the hasp has been sprung. "Curse them, the thieving bastards. May their mothers' milk curdle and turn to blood!" He drops the gun into the empty chest. Touches my shoulder with the whip end. "Come on! Back to camp."

He's back in the wagon seat, curls the whip over the two donkeys, and before I can get in the wagon is rolling.

Anna drives the four-wheeled cart, the bear sprawled out in the rear. I'll walk alongside. Mahmoud follows in the two-wheeler.

I scuff through the sand, limping, but still able to keep up with the plodding donkey. "A good night's sleep, Max," Anna says, "that's what you need." I breathe shallowly; the deep ones stab my ribs.

I hold onto the cart edge for a while. The bear looks at me. A friendly look?

Anna stares at me and I catch her glance. No smile. She's measuring me. Must I fight the bear again? Another test? I could eat her. She has hips, this Anna—in another time—could bear many children. Now—how do you feed children. Her face blurs: complexion like blood and milk. Light-skinned as my sister is dark. With one full breast through her half-open blouse, she nurses a child. A dark child, my sister Genia's child; my sister has no milk—then it's I who am nursing at Anna's breast and I am ashamed.

"Warrior, bear-wrestler. What are you dreaming?"

"Nothing, nothing."

She reins in the donkey, stretches out her hand, and I scramble aboard. Tightly jammed together on the wagon seat.

"You know, Max, a rich Uzbek once offered two camels for me."

"An old man? He needed a third young wife. I'd offer ten horses plus many sheep." Her thigh strikes me. I wince from the ankle pain.

"Not enough, Max. A camel is worth eight yaks, nine horses, or forty-five sheep. I heard this from a trader. Now will you beat the bride price? How many horses? You count better than I can."

"First, I equal the offer. Eighteen horses, then I throw in myself," drop my hand onto her thigh, "a house, chickens, milk cows, more sheep than there are people in the railroad station of Alma Ata and . . ."

"A rouble. Tell me, Max, do you have one rouble?"

I empty my pockets, turn them inside out.

"You're still dressed for a costume ball, Max. In your bear wrestling clothes. Where is the money Golubchek gave you for wrestling the bear?"

"Nothing. He gave me nothing. I thought I was just doing my work. For the circus. For all of us."

"Fool!" She pushes my hand from her thigh. "He always paid Konal. Without the bear wrestling, there is no circus." Her face grows intent, lips narrow. She snaps the reins, shouts, "Ringmaster! Stop!" The donkey ignores her, continues its same slow pace.

Golubchek's back straightens. He sits stiffly for a few moments, then slouches back in the wagon seat.

Snap, snap, snap with her reins. Our donkey begins to edge up on the lead wagon. Twenty feet separate our animal from the chest in the rear. "Ringmaster, we must talk."

Golubchek glances back, waves a hand like he's chasing flies and drives on.

Anna pulls on the left rein and the donkey slowly turns, until it faces the road back to Dzhambul. Mahmoud reins in his cart. On the big wagon goes, lurching through a sandy place. Then it stops. Golubchek looks back. He swings around in his seat. Sits.

Waiting.

The sun is gone. Sky turns purple-black. We sit, surrounded by the twisted saxaul bushes, branches like flat snakes. Frozen in place. Mahmoud's donkey bites his shoulder. He brays. Again, he laughs at us. The bear stirs and drapes its front paws and heavy head over the cart side. The cart sways. A week passes.

Golubchek gets off his wagon. Shoulders swinging, he marches toward us, whip clenched in one fist. "You are in charge, Anna?" he says in a quiet voice.

"You haven't paid the wrestler," she says.

"So?"

"He must be paid."

I see Golubchek's fist clench tighter around the whip handle. I wish for a weapon—a knife, a stick, anything. Look around for a rock.

He's ten feet away. I can see the hairs in one nostril. "You've taught him, this Jew, this cutter of hair, this nothing, and now he wants to be paid." He looks at me, a murderous look. I slide off the wagon seat on the far side, away from him.

"He gets food, this scarecrow of yours. Now he wants to be paid. Like Konal, a real wrestler. And who pays for the clothes that were stolen? Who feeds the brute? Who takes care of all of you?"

"We are nothing, Ringmaster!" She breathes deeply, her breasts assault him-me. "You juggle a few knives. I sit on a trapeze bar. You call this a circus. Juhk is the circus. He can do, might do something unexpected. The great, smart dear bear, Juhk." The last "Jukh" was louder. A command. The bear sits up in the cart, makes a whistling sound, expelling his breath in a whoosh, whoosh. He looks at Anna, turns his great head toward Golubchek.

Golubchek moves closer. Our eyes lock over the wagon sides.

"Juhk obeys me," Anna says. "But he is still a wild beast. So the audience waits . . . for the unexpected . . . for Juhk. . . ."

The bear chomps its jaws, teeth clicking.

"I never told you, Anna, little daughter. I studied at the institute to become a zoo technician, an expert in animal husbandry. We were studying zoology and I said Stalin looked like a walrus. I told my best friend. Only him. He told someone else, a Komsomol who told . . . and out in the cold. I defended myself. A walrus is a noble beast. No use. I should have confessed, begged for mercy." He reaches into his pocket and takes out a fistful of crumpled roubles. "Beg for it, Jew. You are used to living on your knees." He stands there, legs astride, whip in one hand, roubles in the other.

Exaggerating my limp, I walk around the rear of the wagon, up to him, stretch out my hand. He hands me the money. I turn on my heel. Bile in my mouth, a sickness inside. I've asked for my own and lost a friend.

She comes to me that night. Smooth satin skin. Lots of it, like a map of my wandering. A forest of soft hair in my eyes. Twin hills that I kiss, kiss and suck. A deep valley and a wiry thicket that I comb with my fingers. Her hands knead me all over and all the aches and pains begin to leave me. She purrs like a cat, licks my cheek with her tongue and growls, deep little growls from far inside her. I lie beside her, surrounded by all of her, overcome as I've never been before.

And afterwards, we lie together, not daring to talk, make plans, just lie there, waiting for the sun to rise.

When I awaken, I reach out for her. Gone. I look through the screen of gray brush. Only two wagons. The ring is broken. Smoke rises from the *mangalka* and Anna is squatting down, stirring a pot of millet. I get my bowl and walk toward her. She fills my bowl. "Eat, Max, while you can. Mahmoud's gone. While we were entertaining the NKVD, they stole everything. All the costumes, food, except for one bag of millet."

"Where's Golubchek?"

"He went after Mahmoud on foot. He took the pistol. He'll never find the old man."

The millet sticks in my throat. I wash it down with hot green tea.

I get up, grab her hand. "Let's go, Anna. I have five hundred roubles. They're yours. Ours. You defended me yesterday, standing up to the ringmaster like a mother bear defending her cub." I tug her wrist.

"You're not to think that, Max. It's not so. It's you who gave me the courage. I've never stood up to him before."

"To the railroad, Anna. Before he gets back. I'll take you to Alma Ata—my father is there or to my sister in Ili. You'll like her. Or someplace else. Wherever you want to go."

"He'll kill you, Max."

"I know. My eyes are open now. You tried to tell me. I wouldn't see. There is no circus. Just an old bear left and a crazy ringmaster."

"I can't leave him. If we're not here, he'll shoot old Juhk. He's become like the others, my little father. Mahmoud left because Golubchek tried to cheat you. He's turned rotten." She pulls her hand away and sits staring at the earth.

I bend over her, put one hand around her back, one under her legs. "I'll carry you off, carry you all the way to the Dzhambul station." I strain, pull, haul, lift her a foot off the ground, then set her back.

The road one hundred feet from our camp has come alive. Bands of refugees are coming from town and walking toward the station. Everyone thinks another place is better. The bear pounds the cart side with his paws. He must smell the food.

As Anna scoops a portion of millet from the *mangalka*, Golubchek comes striding through the sand, kicking up a dust storm. She places his bowl on the wagon's seat. He approaches the fire, does not look at me, veers away and dashes the millet to the ground with a sweep of his hand.

Anna opens the rear of the cart and Juhk gets down. Rises on his rear legs, stretches and yawns, then ambles toward his pot of millet.

Golubchek sits against the rear wagon wheel. He pulls out a bottle from his coat, drinks.

The bear finishes his meal and begins to root in the sand for Golubchek's millet. The ringmaster's coat falls open. He puts one hand on the pistol butt in his waistband. The bear spits out sand and millet. He growls. Anna hastens toward Juhk, bends over, one arm around his neck. She leads him to a pail of water.

All day, Golubchek sits and drinks, just moving to stay in the shade of the wagon. I talk to Anna in whispers. I find my old rags, put them on. I had left them in the folds of the yurt when I changed into my wrestling costume. Mahmoud, still my friend when he departed with cart and yurt, dropped my clothes in the sand.

Toward sundown, the Uzbek farmer rides toward our camp on his fleshless horse. His sharp eyes take in everything: one missing wagon, old Mahmoud gone. "There is your groom, Anna—look—see—five camels follow him, eighteen horses. He'll barter for you with Golubchek."

"There are no camels," she says.

The Uzbek addresses Golubchek: honeyed words of friendship but we must be gone soon. It's not good for the land, for his sheep to be frightened by the smell of bear. Golubchek sits, head on chest; he does not answer.

The farmer turns his horse and walks it slowly away. I follow him and in the most respectful tone, beg him to stay a while longer, drink our tea. He quickens his pace. Half-running now to catch up, I hand over my white wrestling trousers and shirt. He gives it back. "Praise be to Allah," I say, "we are all his children. Accept our gift and you will be blessed to the end of your days." Now he takes it: we shake hands and he places his hand over his heart in the Uzbek way.

When I return, Golubchek has not stirred. He sits and stares. Anna rests against her bear. How can she? With his fleas and ticks and scratching his balls.

We seem to sit this way for several days, like a sailing ship in the ocean when there is no wind. Anna sleeps near the bear. She does not talk except to urge me to eat.

I sleep fitfully now. I awaken one morning at my grandfather's farm outside Zamoscz. Father and mother have disappeared. They were always leaving, my father trying to get away from the farm, going to Warsaw, to Lublin, until father bought a team of horses, set himself up as a drayman, and carted goods from the railroad sidings to the wholesalers in Zamoscz.

A large boil began to grow on my left jawbone. It

grew infested, angry and swollen. I became sick and couldn't eat. Grandfather bundled me up and carried me into his wagon. We set off on a dark, moonless night. Savage birds swooped down and flew about Grandfather's head. Tried to peck at me. I huddled against him, face tormented, throat so tight, I could not swallow. Then we pulled up before the witch's house, a woman famed for casting the evil eye. We used to tear branches from the twisted apple tree in her yard and use them to frighten the smaller children, called these sticks witch's wood. For a few kopecks, she would predict the sex of an unborn child, rub black ashes on a pregnant woman's belly to aid the birthing, or sell a potion so powerful that a Talmud scholar, a handsome man, would, once imbibing this mixture, fall in love with an ugly woman. Or so my father told me years later.

The old witch had died and the village women washed and dressed her and laid her out. My grandfather held my hand and led me into her hovel. He dragged me into the dark room while I kicked, howled, and threw myself on the floor. He laid the cold hand of the corpse on my left cheek. For a long while afterwards, I feared the dark.

When my parents returned to the farm, a bitter quarrel started up between my father and his father-in-law. My father cursed the old one, called him an ignorant donkey, packed us up, and never returned. He took me to a doctor in Lublin who lanced the boil. I still bear a tiny scar on my cheekbone.

Then when I left him—Ruvin Chaim Schmulovicz —my own father—he said to me, "You were born

with a full head of black hair. A miracle! Now you
want to be a soldier? You'll lose your head!" He
meant well, my old man. But I didn't listen. And my
son, if I ever have one—will he listen to me. And if he
does, what will I tell him?

I awaken from a restless sleep, partly covered by
sand. Like in a dream, my father comes to me, "Go
Mendele, run away. You remember I ran from the
Germans, saved us all—the ones who stayed behind
are bones and ashes."

Like a snake, I slither along the sand, creeping
toward Anna's body, curled in sleep next to a wagon
wheel. Sand gets into my trouser waistband; enters
the hole in my pants above the knee. I throw one arm
around her sleeping form. "Shah, Anna. Not a
sound. We're marooned here." I grasp her forearm,
stroke it, bend over and kiss her ear, bite the earlobe,
stick my tongue into the shell, lick her ear clean of
sand. "We must leave before it gets any lighter. The
circus will sink beneath the sands. It's finished, you
said so."

"All right," she says in a furry voice.

"Take extra clothing," I tell her, "anything you
have for trade. I have nothing, came with nothing,
leave the same way."

She rolls a few things into a blanket, knots the ends
and throws it over one shoulder. Then she plops
down on the sand. "I must say good-bye to poor old
Juhk."

I get down on my knees. "No, no, Anna. Please,
no time," and hook my arm under hers, pull her to
her feet. The bear grunts, coughs. Golubchek doesn't
stir. I hope he's sleeping off another drunk.

We are on the road and walking fast. I jump up and down, pound myself to ward off the morning chill.

I lead Anna around the small settlement at the edge of Dzhambul station. The sun is up. The station here is only a plain wooden building. Refugees are scattered around the shelter of its walls. Some stir, rub their eyes. Others wait at the water spout, pushing and elbowing to fill their buckets. Will she follow me, I wonder. Anna hasn't spoken for an hour. I finger the five hundred roubles in my pants pocket. My circus wages.

"Come Anna, the vendors are setting up." I tug her arm. She follows me, dragging her feet. When I slow down, she remains a few steps behind. I buy a clasp knife with a long thin blade; I'll never be without a knife again. Two hundred roubles. Then I buy a melon, slice it open, give Anna half and sink my teeth into the red-fleshed pulp. At least she's eating now. "Here, finish my piece," she says. I stop before an Uzbek crone, a jumble of colored scarfs in her basket. I draw one out, a many colored silk from China. Hold it up. "Do you like this one?" Anna shrugs. "Seventy-five roubles," the woman announces. "You'll take fifty," and I shove fifty roubles in her hand. I tie the scarf around Anna's neck.

"It's pretty, and you can tie it over your nose and mouth, keep out the sand when it blows. How did you ever do without one?"

"I did without many things," she answers in a low voice. "A mother. I never had a mother. Just Golubchek. His hair is gray-streaked now. A young, strong man when I traveled with him. I had many mothers then: they came and went. A bareback rider, an Intourist guide who said she was a voice teacher, then a trapeze artist. The girl could do a triple somersault. You've seen that long scar on Golubchek's wrist, a brother cut him, the girl's brother because Golubchek walked by night. . . ."

"I walk by day with you, Anna. You know *that*."

"What does it matter now? He brained him with a club."

"Who brained who?"

"Golubchek brained the trapeze girl's brother, knocked him senseless, then the whole family of aerialists left us . . . they were Mongols but Russified."

"Come Anna, you'll tell me the rest on the train. I hear it coming."

She doesn't move, pulls on the new scarf around her neck.

I look toward the tracks. "There's still time," I say soothingly. "That's the train to Samarkand. I've had enough of hot places. We'll wait, go the other way, back to Alma Ata, a good climate there, apples, peaches, beautiful fruit, family, my family, you'll love it."

"First, I must buy you something, Max." Only a handful of vendors here, not a regular market place. She walks and now I follow. I buy some flat Kazakh bread, a few apples for the train, push roubles into the vendor's hand and hurry after Anna. She turns when I catch up to her and claps an Uzbek skull cap on my head. "Wear this, Max, you can almost pass for a tribesman with your dark skin."

Impractical these little hats, they don't stay on, good for a Chassid in a synagogue. For me, useless, but I kiss her on both cheeks, promise to wear it forever.

She glances away, a faraway look, back to the road.

"No one is following. Besides, here at the station there are many people, militia. He'd not dare attack me."

"Come, Max," she says. "I have no picture of you, no remembrance. I want your photograph."

A refugee, a European stands at the edge of the station with a tripod and large black camera. Nearby, an Uzbek youth holds the lead of a one-humped camel. Camels, pictures—I must humor her like a pregnant woman.

So I step up to the photographer. "Twenty-five roubles for your picture," he says. "I can develop it in five minutes. You and your *galiebta* together, only forty roubles and for both of you, on the camel, fifty roubles."

"Money thrown out, Anna. We need bread. Who needs pictures!" I turn to her, grasp both her arms. "We have each other; that's better than any picture. Let me hold your bundle." I reach for it and she says, "No, I can carry it." A shifty look toward the road.

"Make up your minds," the photographer says. "I'm a busy man, can't wait all day." The camel makes a slobbering sound, stretches his long neck as I look into his dumb eyes. He spits on my forehead. The Uzbek boy pulls on the camel's bit and brings him to his knees. Anna mounts the saddle behind his single hump. The camel rises to his full height. Anna is not looking into the camera; she scans the horizon as the photographer ducks under his shroud and snaps her picture. She laughs, the first time today, and slides off the beast, then stands near the camel and gives her circus bow. I refuse to get on. She swings me around by the shoulders to face the camera and pulls me to her with her left hand; a strong embrace and the cameraman slips under his black cloth and snaps again. First a wrestler, now a movie star I have become, in torn rags and running from a bear and crazy ringmaster.

Now we must wait. An eternity. The photographer ducks into a small yurt. I hear the train. Waiting. In the open. I want to mingle with the crowd. Lose us. "Come out," I shout, "let's have those pictures. We must go!" The photographer emerges holding two prints in his fingers, waving them in the air. I grab them, give him his cursed roubles. I won't look at the stupid pictures. Anna takes them from me, stuffs them into her bosom.

I hook her arm and head for the train. Words tumble out, "He swam after me in the Volga or the Don . . . who can remember . . . so many rivers . . . so many towns . . . I was doing the wash on a rickety low pier. . . ."

"Come along, Anna," I pull her. A dead weight.

"Gossiping with the other women, when part of the pier broke off . . . and laundry and I and pier, now raft started to float down the river. I can barely swim. If he hadn't come along then and seen me, my little father . . . he ran along the shore faster than the current, then threw himself in and swam toward

me . . . held me on the raft . . . swept along
. . . for miles . . . his body protecting mine. . . ."

I can't listen to her. While she babbles on, I am in
the Garden of Eden, a naked full-fleshed Anna
surrounded by bears, tigers, many camels—I push
through the animals, trying to reach her—I'm
dressed in rags—she retreats into a grove of apples,
grows smaller, apples rain on my head, I slip, get up,
hard to walk on apples, apples everywhere.

She screams, a hoarse cry, starts to run.

I chase after her, grab her around the waist, dig my
heels into the sand.

A cloud of dust beside the road. It's the great
brown bear! He's coming fast and refugees, tribes-
men, donkey carts scatter from in front of his path.

I hang on to Anna. Her ass in my face, my hands
digging into her waist, surround her; my cock rises,
salutes her backside. She twists and bends my
interlocking fingers, breaks my hold and runs again.

An open truck careens around the depot, blocking
my view of the bear. Two soldiers on the truck, rifles
unslung. I'm on Anna again, caught her. Take her
down with a quick tug on an ankle. My skull cap falls
on her belly. She kicks loose, yells, "Juhk, Juhk!" I
hear automatic rifle fire. She's back on her feet, can't
hold her. I grab her around the waist, slip, hang on to
her hips. She strikes back with her elbow, catches me
on the ear. Rifle fire. She squirms around, faces me,
bangs my temple with her fist—once, twice. The bear
looms closer. Juhk smashes into a cart, keeps going.

I'm straining Anna to me, smothered in her
breasts. She rains short hard blows to my ribs. I

snatch a look over her shoulder. The bear is up on hind legs now. Bullets fly, hit the sand. The bear circles a file of camels and the pursuing truck changes direction. Anna knees me in the balls. I double over. A fist smashes against the side of my jaw. She could beat my old friend Berchik—I duck—boxing champion of Zamoscz. She rains blows to my head, ribs: I lose count. Another blow to my cheekbone and I'm flat on my back. I struggle to my knees, then fall on my face.

The army truck bears down on Juhk. He charges the truck, the brave one. Crumples. The truck halts and the two soldiers pour lead into his body.

Anna throws herself onto her bear. I pass out. I awaken, stand on shaky legs. Ha, ha, ha, ha. There she is, my beloved. Even beat the wrestling champion of Bulgaria—that's what Golubchek called me. Can't stop laughing. Dizzy, fall to my knees. A dry wind rising, sand swirls five feet in the air. A black car pulls up near the fallen Juhk. Three four-letter men get out. Another truck masks my view.

Which way?

Toward my beloved Anna, boxing champion of Uzbekistan?

Or away?

I start to crawl on hands and knees. I'm laughing and crawling.

Which way?

Can't see through the rising sandstorm.

So I crawl. My stomach hurts and suddenly I vomit and spill yellow bile and specks of red-fleshed melon to the sand. I change directions, not to track through the mess.

Which direction now?
I creep like an infant.
I laugh; I can't stop laughing.
The dry wind blows from the west. Sand stings my
face, rises ten, fifteen feet in the air.
It will cover us all.

SIX

I hang around the Dzhambul station for four days watching for Anna. Waiting. Eat a few handfuls of millet and hot water from the station spout. She never comes and I am afraid to return to our camp with a clasp knife and face the ringmaster and his pistol. I am a little ashamed.

Still I stay on.

I dig a small hollow in the sand, stretch out and try to sleep and not think about food. Open my eyes and see a gray cat circling around me. "Come here, kitty, kitty."

She comes closer, looks at me curiously, that Madam; skin and bones. I try some cat noises and she inches closer; almost I can reach out and touch her. I creep along the sand, raise one hand and slowly bring it down on her head and begin scratching her behind the ears. Grab her by the right leg, lift her into the air, knife in its belly, long cut, blood, guts fall out, gray and yellow. I skin the gray fur, slice meat from its thin sides and roast the strips over a fire.

My father stares at me from the dying embers. It's all right, son, it's not kosher, but it's all right. YOU WILL LIVE!

The next morning, I vomit and lie sick in the sand next to the station all day. I don't even have the strength to crawl out of the sun. At night, I drag myself to the water spout and beg a station worker for a drink. I drink a liter, vomit green and yellow, then nothing comes up and I fall into a dead sleep, knife open at my side.

I awaken just as my slipper is being gently removed from my left foot. I grope for the knife in the sand, close my hand on the haft, push myself up with my other hand. Startled, the thief sits back on his haunches. I lunge, knife goes through his shirt; I draw the knife blade down; it cuts into his padded vest.

"Eat cat, eat cat!" I scream as he crawls away. He didn't even run off like a proper thief; crawls in the sand, leaves a trail like a snake. I look at the knife, blood on the tip and I put the knife to my lips, suck the tip and lap the edge of the blade with my tongue.

I trade my slippers for a piece of Kazakh bread. While eating, I reach into one pocket, close my hand on the knife; then in the other pocket I feel the barber's tools in my sack. Trace the outlines: razor, soap, whetstone. If I ever sell my knife or tools, I'll be like the others, thousands all around me; they beg, beg, then die.

No more trade goods. Weak, I am weak, can barely walk. I go from one group of refugeees to another in ever widening circles, fall down, get up. Two apples. Walk on. A man-woman pair, Jews, two children, a grandmother, I hold out cupped hands, *"Essen, essen."*

"Poor devil," the grandmother says, reaching into her pack. The man scowls. She hands me a piece of hard bread, cheese, a handful of dates. I take it and walk away, to eat alone, under a saxaul bush.

I'm too tired to go for water. Before I lie down, I handle my knife in my left pocket and the barber's sack in my right. I hollow out a place in the sand and fall asleep.

Awaken, still dark and I must relieve myself. I head away from my nest, keep the bush in sight, so I can return. Stumble and fall headlong. Push myself up and my foot kicks back, hits a softness. I turn on my knees, run my hands over the mound. A body. I place my ear near his mouth—no breath. Feel his heart through his quilted jacket. Sit back to rest and my hand strikes a piece of cloth. An Uzbek yarmulke. I put it on. Then I strip his upper body and listen again for a heartbeat. Not a sound. My luck has turned. I throw off my clothes. Pull on the dead one's long wide trousers and over them, his long robe. As it

grows lighter, I look closely at the man's face. Middle-
aged. What killed him? He's not starved. A disease?
Typhus? Must chance it. He's a Tadzhik, I am sure.
Dark black beard, dark complexioned and a strong
chin. He could pass for a European, so with my beard
perhaps I can pass for a Tadzhik. On my knees, I
work the rings off his fingers. Scoop out a sandy
grave, start to roll him in. Stop and dress him in my
old rags. In he goes. Pull off his soft leather boots and
wool socks. Fine quality. Make room for his feet with
more digging. Cover him up. Smooth out the sand.

I head back for the Dzhambul station. Good-bye,
barber. From the first vendor I can find, I barter a ring
for a savory mix of meat, carrots, and rice. Bread.
Lots of bread. Hot green tea. I am reviving.

I head for the water spout beside the station, strip
off my clothes and take a good wash. Try to comb my
beard, my hair with my fingers. Foolish, I have a
comb in my kit. I must get on the train. Go some
place. Anywhere. Away from Anna and her fists,
away from the ringmaster. To hell with them! If I were
not so hungry, I could have bargained with the ring I
gave up for one good meal. No matter. I have another
ring and fine soft well-fitting leather boots.

By the time I have cleaned myself up, the area
around the station has become a small bazaar. Refu-
gees are trading clothes, pans, anything for food.
One vendor stirs a savory soup in a large kettle.
Another sells sweet, soft cheese. A man in a donkey
cart drives up with a load of stinking, cured fish. The
Kazakhs drink *kumiss*; the Uzbeks drink their *aizan*,
pot cheese mixed with water.

A crowd is gathering around a tall blond Russian in

a long leather coat, so he must be an important official. The refugees all talk at once, while he looks down at them coldly. I join them and using my elbows, work my way toward the Russian. He writes a name in a little book and waves that man off. I hear him say, "We need factory experience, men who can run sewing machines, drill presses, or lathes."

"Comrade Excellency," I address him, "I can sew uniforms, shoes, whatever you need."

"You scarecrow? Can you read directions in Russian?"

"Yes, I can read a Russian newspaper."

With one big lie and one truth, I become a contract worker. No longer a scrounging, thieving refugee, but a worker. Once on the train and underway, I am well fed with bread, salami, and cheeses. Each one of us is given a ladle for getting hot water at the station spouts. Plenty of tea. I save bread for an afternoon snack. The blond Russian, Yanek, places us in three compartments, about twenty-five men, and all during the two-day trip, he wanders from compartment to compartment—a quick count—calls out our names from the little book—a news bulletin—our boys have thrown them back again—soon all Soviet territory will be in our hands—and out he goes.

In Siberia, when it was forty degrees below zero, and padded pants, quilted jacket, and every rag we could find and stuff in between, layer upon layer of rags, did no good, we froze in our tracks on the way to the logging. On such a day, when a man could not work in the woods, the commandant might let us turn back and spend the day in our huts.

Cold. The wind blew through every chink in the logs. We tamped rags, dirt scraped from the floor with our knives, straw, anything to keep out the drafts, then lay down in all our outdoor clothing, four men huddled together, all our blankets and overcoats piled on top of us. Someone always said, they can't exile us from Siberia.

And now I am on my way back. But not all the way. Just to Semipalatinsk, northernmost city in Kazakhstan on the Novosibirsk railway line, at the edge of the Siberian taiga.

Anna is gone. Yet I see her face reflected in every dirty railway car window as we pass through dark tunnel after tunnel, on our way north.

She must have loved me very much to have raised such large purple bruises on my left cheek.

Semipalatinsk. The city is floating in mud.

Almost June now, and as I walk through the streets, the thaw has thrown up garbage: a broken sled, a dog's body crawling with white maggots, a child's wagon. A Tatar boy stands on dry ground and with a long stick, he tries to push the wagon out of the mud. And worst of all, the stench from the untreated cesspools. A Gehenna of smells!

I am quartered in an old stable; six men in two horse stalls. Sleep on damp straw.

Ahh . . . the wonderful food at the workers' canteen! I and the other contract workers get chits and with mine I buy meat dumplings, delicious hot stew of lamb, rice, and carrots, strong cabbage soup. Black bread. I can't get filled up. Always, I take some extra bread and stow it in a pocket to eat in the late evening.

Then I am assigned to a barracks in a red brick building, three stories high, formerly a slaughter-house. The road is named Sand Street. All the streets are sandy and white in Siberia, the spring thaw drags on for weeks; in this soil, the water quickly drains away.

There are mostly refugees here: Ukrainians, Poles, Jews. In the cafeteria, one girl, thin, straw-colored hair, with a slight limp, takes good care of me. Without asking, she ladles an extra portion into my bowl. For three meals, she moves in front of another dark girl and fills my bowl to overflowing. The fourth meal I look for her but she is not there and my portion is halved.

"Comrade," she says on the fifth day, ladle of thick soup held over my bowl, "I must speak to you. Later, not here. You remind me of someone."

She's really too thin for my taste, a pretty face however; only a girl-woman, with little buds on her chest.

As I leave my quarters the next morning, a man comes up to me and roughly grasps my shoulder. "Where have you been? What kept you?" He wears a black turtleneck sweater and his left arm is in a sling.

"For five nights, I've been in a horse's stall."

"I'm Teodorov, the Bulgarian. Yanek promised me a man who could read Russian."

"Who is Yanek? I can read Russian."

"Who is Yanek, he asks. He brought you here. The man in the long leather coat. He fed you like a king.

How will we win this war? Such disorganization!" He claps his hands to his forehead. "Chaos! Bureaucratic fumbling. Ink souls every one!" He fumbles in a back pocket, draws out a tattered piece of paper and looks at his list. "Ah, the shoe factory, that's the place. I know you know nothing. But you can read. Follow me." He walks with long strides and I quicken my steps to stay with him.

Within two blocks, we come to a long, low concrete building. Inside, a clattering whirring of machinery. Piles of hides on the floor. Teodorov leads me to a man who is bent over a sewing machine, a wrench in his hand. The man looks up. "Lenin was a smart man, Teodorov. In 1926 he made the New Economic Policy and traded with the Americans for sewing machines. These are better than the old Pfaff machines from Germany."

"Marvelous," Teodorov answers. "Americanski machines came all the way to Kazakhstan. Now put away your tools, please, Levitsky. Here is your new man. Train him. Explain to him everything. The whole job. Educate him."

Levitsky straightens up, folds his arms and recites.

"The Work. Clickers cut the leather. An operator puts the pieces together, called an upper maker. That's you," and he points his finger at me. "A shoemaker puts the uppers on a last and fastens the uppers to the soles." He hardly takes a breath. "Mostly women's shoes made here."

"Good, very good explaining." Teodorov says. "He reads the papers. Start today," as he turns away and waves good-bye.

"De bist fun inserer?" Levitsky says in Yiddish. I nod.

"You're not a shoemaker, stand up too straight," and he takes my hand between his two hands and shakes it up and down. "Now fifteen to twenty uppers is the quota; twenty-five to thirty and you are a Stakhanovite. He's a good man, the Bulgarian."

He leads me to a machine and sits down at the bench in front of it. "Look, watch—I'll go slow." He places two pieces of leather under the needle and starts to pump the treadle with his right food. "You see, now you try it. Sometimes we make boots to special order for the commissars. Oh what I would give to make one beautiful pair of ladies' shoes instead of these ugly ones."

I sit down in his place. The leather jams. "Not so fast," he says. "Pull it out carefully, don't break the needle and start again."

I pump slowly and stitch the two pieces together. "Go on working. I'll be back later."

The time flies, I hardly look up from the machine and he is back. "Three pieces will do. Poor workmanship, but they will do." The fourth, he cuts apart with his knife and puts the pieces back on the pile in front of me. "Here are some chits for the week. Go to lunch, pay you will get next week. See me here after lunch and you will read to the workers' class."

A good beet soup for lunch and the girl with the straw-colored hair slips me an extra hunk of bread, with a quick look around to see if they are watching.

In the factory, Levitsky leads me past the shoemakers pounding on the lasts to a small room, opens the door and sits me down on a chair. Eight men sit opposite; four on one bench, four on another. He says, "This is Max, your new teacher."

The pupils stare at me, arms folded. I stare back. We stay this way, no one talking for about fifteen minutes, seems like hours, and then are called back to work.

The next day I finish ten uppers that are acceptable and again sit silently after lunch with my pupils.

I am at the end of the food line that evening when the blond girl appears. I take a better look at her: a pretty turned-up nose and pointy chin. She motions to me and I take my bowl to an empty table in the back. She sits across from me.

"Eat first, Max, we can talk later."

I drop the spoon. "You know me?"

"You are the finest, the best, the most generous man I have ever met."

"Not me." I bend my head and attack the soup. I tear off chunks of bread. When I look up at her, she stares into my eyes.

"You fed us, you defended us when the kolkhozniks attacked our Jewish settlement, you. . . ." She reaches into her pocket and puts a handful of dates on the table.

"So who are you?"

"The daughter of Chaya and Yitzhak."

"Of course, ah . . . and how you've grown." I pop a date into my mouth. "You must be fourteen, fifteen."

"I'm seventeen."

"Your mother? Father?"

"My father died three months after you left. My mother married the baker two weeks afterwards. The bitch!"

"I'm sorry, very sorry. She seemed a good woman. Why are you so angry?"

"Two weeks! Like a bitch in heat! And to him, that coward, always buttering up to them—the masters. I must get back to work."

I watch her as she walks away. Drags a foot. From the back, one could almost mistake her for a woman.

At the next day's study session, Teodorov turns up, a newspaper in his hand. "Now our lessons will begin. First I must tell you Ukrainians that some of your people are filthy, rotten collaborators with the enemy and you can distinguish yourselves here, restore your honor—although I am sure you are all loyal Soviet citizens—by performing like Stakhanovites and turning out twenty-five percent above your quota. You will be rewarded. And you, our Polish brothers," he pauses, a shifting of feet from the pupils, two drop their hands to their side, "you, too, have little to be proud of. Now our glorious Russian troops are advancing on the enemy and will soon cross the Polish border. They will restore the country to the workers, and you, too, can exceed the quotas and redeem your country's honor. Next week, I will lecture on the different ethnic groups and tribes of our glorious Soviet Socialist Republic. Read to them, Comrade Max," and he turns on his heels, begins to whistle a tune as he strides away.

I read from *Pravda*. "The victorious Russian army is

advancing on all fronts. Vitebsk has fallen, Bobruisk and Mogilev have been liberated. Three German divisions are encircled in the Minsk area. . . ."

By the late afternoon, I have finished fifteen uppers. Levitsky says four are rotten, rejects them; six more, poor work, but it is good for a Jew to point the way, so he will pass eleven by.

I have not seen the girl for a few days. While I am eating my soup that night, I see her approaching, carrying a battered samovar. She sits down, places her cup near mine and fills both cups with tea and puts a hard cake beside each cup. "You know what she said to me, the bitch?" I see scabs on her scalp, probably from lice bites. "When I pleaded with her to wait, she said, 'You are not good looking, and with that limp, you are lucky if you can find a man who will have you. Try to find one to take care of you. Don't be too choosy. I've found mine and you're on your own.' The bitch!"

I can't believe Chaya would talk that way to her daughter but. . . .

The girl talks on. "You noticed I'm crippled."

I put my hand on her shoulder, slide down her sweatered arm, and then at the elbow bulge where her sleeves are rolled up, I stop. "You walk just fine. Like a lady. You are not crippled."

"I fell from the apple tree in front of our hut. Remember it? Did she try to get a doctor? Did she? No! She said it would heal by itself."

I run my hand over her elbow, caress her bare arm, then trap her fist under my hand. "No more. Shah, shah. Keep still."

"You're a good man, Max. I never met a man like you."

"I'm rotten. What did you say your name is?"

"I won't tell you my old name. I've taken a new name—Bronya. Come. I can get off early. I'll show you where I live."

A warm breeze blows across my face tonight. Spring, long delayed in this cold city on the border of Siberia, must come some time.

She leads me through the muddy streets. A house leans crazily to one side as if it has not recovered from the winter frost and wind. A man on a ladder nails a piece of sheet metal back on his roof. Next door, a woman sweeps the dirt floor of her hut and with strong sweeping gestures, chases the dirt over her doorsill. I take the girl's hand and we walk in silence. At a large puddle, she hesitates and before she can skirt around it, I sweep my hand around her back, lift her up, how light she is, and slosh through the water while her feet dance in the air.

She stops before a hut with a geranium in each window. Draws me inside. Pink curtains on the window, like fine underwear. She closes them. A room with four beds, one on each wall, hooks on the walls near each bed and a crude stove—roughly plastered rocks in a square pattern, a hunk of iron across the top and a stovepipe to the roof, badly fitted in. I can see light, a single star between stovepipe and ceiling.

"Do you want a drink?" Bronya says, taking off her coat and hanging it on a hook near the bed on the right. "Give me your coat. I'll hang it next to mine."

Now with my eyes more accustomed to the darkness, I can see that one bed has someone in it, someone huge because the blanket covers a large mound.

"Where is our vodka?" Bronya addresses the blanket. She pushes me gently to sit down on the bed.

The blanket is pulled higher and bare feet appear at one end of the bunk opposite. Two feet, no three—four!

Giggles, laughter, the blanket squirms.

Bronya bends down to a small cabinet near the back bed and opens it. "Inger, where did you hide the vodka?"

"Under my bed, *liebchen*. Don't drink it all. Just because you captured a man with a beard is no reason to drink it all."

Bronya reaches under the bed and comes up with a bottle. She gets two glasses and hands them to me, pours two drinks, a larger and a smaller one.

The blanket turns, twists, jumps, a knee hits the wall with a rat-ta-ta-tat like the hoofbeats of a Polish hussar. Rat-ta-ta-tat, rat-ta-ta-tat. Then a blond close-cropped head appears. "He's bashful," she pats the blanket, "won't come out. What a nice young man you've found, darling Bronya. It's getting dark, light a candle so I can see him better."

Bronya gives me her glass to hold and lights a candle in a saucer atop the iron stove.

Two bare arms reach out from under the blanket. "Come closer to the light, man with the black beard. I'm not properly dressed or I'd get up, and him," she taps the blanket, "he doesn't want to catch a chill. So please come closer."

I sip my vodka. A good burn.

"You are the first one with Bronya," Inger says. "Believe me. The other girls have no pride. Ten women here for every man. They'll take up with grandfathers, legless veterans or sheep. No shame. But this one," she slaps the blanket harder, "he's young and his wife . . ." A hairy arm shoots out and pulls Inger under the blanket. Now there are four legs, no doubt about it. Two hairy ones, gnarled toes and two fine woman's legs and knees too.

"She's a Volga German," Bronya says, "but hates the Nazis."

I know of them, taken from their land and shipped here when the war started. But never close to one of them. She looks like anyone else.

More laughter from under the blanket. A man's gruff voice, says Inger, Inger, Inger.

Is that all he can say, I wonder. I try to guess his nationality. The blanket gets very active now, rises and falls like a wave coming toward shore. I place my arm around Bronya's thin shoulders. She shivers, rests her head on my shoulder. I could fall back with her on the bed; it would be so easy. Yet I have a different kind of desire. I protect her, this child. Join my other hand to my elbow, so I encircle her body. And what does she want? Like all the others? I am rising, faintly stirring, then it stops. She makes so much of me. Treats me like a hero, like a brother. My desire ebbs. Still it is good to sit here and hold her while the candle burns down slowly. The blanket is quiet, only heavy snoring from its depths. A dark head appears, turns to the wall; blonde head next to it, arm thrown over the man next to her. The blanket slips down, white shoulders gleam.

The candle flickers. I hold Bronya. I tighten my grip. The candle goes out. I can't let her go. We lean back, slide back on the bed, backs against the wall. I am drowsy, but I can't let her go. I don't want to let her go.

I can hardly keep my eyes open at the machine the following day. The work is rotten. I've lost all my new skills. By lunch time, I've only finished four uppers, lucky if I do ten by day's end.

The Bulgarian stands before us in the classroom. He waves *Pravda*, but doesn't hand it to me. "Faster! You must meet the quotas. Our soldier-comrades need shoes!" He's forgotten we are turning out ugly brown women's shoes. "Work like Stakhanovites, work like patriots. Work like you are defending Stalingrad. Work! Work!" He almost jumps into the air at the last "work."

"Now for my lecture on the many Soviet peoples. You know we are composed of many different peoples all welded into one fighting socialist army. We are Russians, Tatars, Cossacks, Uzbeks, Kazakhs, Georgians, Siberian Yakuts, and the reindeer herdsman, the tiny tribe of Chukchi, only a few thousand, and many other peoples, Jews, too, all under the glorious banner of the Soviet Socialist Republic. Now there is no tribe better than another. Some of the bureaucrats from Great Russia look down on all those who are not Great Russians. They look down on the native Siberians, the people whom we are leading out of darkness and the people who have joined us in the struggle for the survival of the Great Soviet Socialist Republic. This is wrong! Wrong!" He pounds his fist into the palm of his hand. "That's all. Back to work. No time for the newspaper today. Shoes for the army of the Soviet Socialist Republic. Your mission!" He hums a tune, turns and sings a few bars of a song and always in a hurry, he is gone.

Levitsky comes over later while I am pumping away at the treadle. "Did you hear the song he sang," he whispers into my ear. "*Dremlen Feygl Af Di Tsvagn,*'Birds Are Drowsing on the Branches.' Could he be one of us?"

I shrug, won't be drawn in.

"Is that all you can do, young man? Raise your shoulders? Ever since he came, we have had more Jews placed in the factory. He must be one of us."

"He's a Bulgarian," I answer.

The days and nights take on a pattern. Work on uppers, read from *Pravda*, sometimes *Izvestia*, see Bronya in the evening, and once a week although not on the same day, Comrade-Professor Teodorov the Bulgarian gives a lecture.

One day, I make my quota and Levitsky does not have to undo a single upper.

A hot day that Saturday and Bronya begs me to take her swimming in the river. I have no bathing suit, I tell her. She has sewn up a new suit and models it for me in her room.

She parades up and back; how thin she is in the flowered suit, yet she forgets her limp. I kiss her. I must—I want to, pressing her to my chest. Her heart pounds like a pigeon I once held in both hands in the old country.

I cut the legs off my oldest pants, save the cloth with the old habit of a refugee, as if anyone would trade for two cut-off pants legs.

The sun strikes hard as we start for the Irtysk River. Bronya carries our lunch wrapped in an old shirt and she places a binoculars with only one eyepiece around my neck. "Now you look like a proper tourist," she says.

On the way, we pass other couples, walking hand in hand: old men with young girls, two girls walking together, a girl with a one-armed veteran. Bronya says, "I feel so lucky to have a whole young man at my side."

At the glass-topped open air shower, I hold the lunch while Bronya gets under the water inside the stall; then she holds the binoculars and I get under the spray. We cool off as the water dries from our clothing.

Then Bronya wets two pieces of cloth, knots the ends and makes hats for both of us. A relief to let her think for me. My girl-woman is smart.

When the bridge over the Irtysk comes into sight, a train, black smoke trailing, is starting to cross the trestle. Two soldiers with rifles guard the near end of the bridge.

We draw closer and I idly take off the binoculars and with one eye, I pick out the winding river, the place where I see people going down the bank to the right of the bridge—then I train the glasses on the tail end of the train. Through the one eye, a muzzle points at me, as big as a cannon. The soldier stands in firing position. I grab Bronya's hand, drop to the ground, pull her down with me and throw myself over her. "Don't move, Bronya!"

"Max, Max, let me up, you're choking me!"

"Lie still." I throw the binoculars as far away as I can. I ease myself off her chest, hold her down with one hand and wait for the shots.

Wait, wait. They never come.

I let her up and we sit side by side in the sand. "Let's go home, Bronya darling. I'm a fool. When I looked through the binoculars, a soldier must have seen me, trained his gun on me. Why didn't he fire?"

Bronya looks as if she is about to cry. "We've come so far . . . it's so hot. . . ."

I pull her to her feet and arm in arm, we walk toward the bank where the others have disappeared over the edge. The soldiers pay no attention to me; no one comes forth to arrest me.

As I help her down the steep bank, it comes to me: the strangeness of living among them. A man can be arrested, held for a week, then released. For the same offense, another is jailed for three months and when his term is up, he is resentenced for three more years. One never knows the rules of their game.

I hold her up in the water. She can't swim, but she trusts me. Then Bronya gets out and rests on the bank.

I swim lazily out and around and back and out again. Always when I look toward shore, Bronya is watching for me. I do not fight the river like I swam the river crossings in Poland. I become one with the

Siberian Irtysk, rest in its arms and it is the best swim I have ever had in my life.

Teodorov storms into our classroom; Levitsky trailing behind. "You are not meeting the quotas. Levitsky, you too are responsible."

Levitsky, behind Teodorov, says, "Other factories have electricity, electric driven machines and . . ."

"Silence, parasite! You, too, Teacher, and you eight men in this room, are more responsible than the eighty men in this factory, you eight have the special privilege of an hour's study every day. Soviet justice can be swift and hard! Now I'll tell you a story about the Cossacks. Any Cossacks here?"

A young mustachioed man, who sits on the bench like a horseman, taps his chest.

Teodorov takes a deep breath, adjusts his sling. "I have not always liked the Cossacks. The backbone of Rangel's White Army. Counterrevolutionary dogs! But a Cossack on horseback, a Red Cossack on our side is worth ten ordinary men. The Bulgarians are mighty wrestlers and we . . ." He claps his hand to his forehead. "I am wandering again, comrades; one of my faults. The Cossack saber is thunder and lightning."

"I saw one Cossack—ours—riding at a gallop at a German officer who tried to raise his pistol. The Cossack neatly cut him into three parts with one stroke: head and shoulders, half the body and an arm, and all the rest of him."

The Cossack tugs his mustache and stands erect. "I am Yermak, son of Alexei. Comrade Teodorov, you tell us everyone must be treated alike. The tribesmen, the Poles, even the Jews are just like us.

"But isn't it so, comrade, that while all these people if they understand and support the revolution are good people, even the Jews as you said, but some people are better than others. There are no stronger, fiercer, more loyal fighters for the Soviet Republic than the Red Cossacks!"

"You're a fool, Yermak. No, not a fool, you lack revolutionary understanding. If the Cossacks are so great, why did the Germans knife through the Ukraine, a Cossack stronghold, like a thresher through a wheatfield?"

"We were taken by surprise," the Cossack answers.

"Could you Cossacks alone have saved Moscow, Leningrad and all the other great cities? No! Because alone, comrade, you are nothing, just a twig to be broken." He reaches into his coat pocket and takes out a pencil and snaps it between his finger. "Put all those twigs together, all the forty, fifty nationalities of our great Republic—and you have a mighty tree . . .

"And no one . . ."

"No one can bring it down."

Later when I am back at the machine, Levitsky comes over and asks, "Well, Max, are they learning anything, your pupils?"

"Who knows? A Cossack Jew-hater talked today for the first time."

"So?"

"I wish I had my knife. I'd feel safer."

"Not in the factory, Max, not . . . shah, here he comes."

Teodorov claps Levitsky and me on the shoulder,

almost draws us to him. "They are beginning to talk.
The eight in that room are the worst scum—Siberia
would be too good for them. That young Cossack is a
killer. In the retreat from the Ukraine, Yermak passed
through his own village. Some Whites had killed his
father and escaped. One of the murderers was his
cousin. Yermak fired his uncle's house, sabered
uncle, aunt, and two young nephews, one a boy of
five."

"He's a sloppy worker," Levitsky says. "I expect
him to fly from the factory anyday. Who brought him
here?"

"He does not think he did anything wrong."
Teodorov looks at Levitsky and then at me. "He's
proud of his butchery. We will save him, Teacher. A
wild animal, but loyal to the Soviet State. I am talking
too much. Back to work," and with a clap on my
back, he is off.

Just before quitting time, Teodorov returns and
stands next to me. I pretend I do not see him and
continue working on the machine.

"Stop work, Max," he says. "Tomorrow there will
be no *Pravda*. Become a real teacher. Talk to them.
Make them talk, the devils. You have one there,
Danov by name. He killed a Lithuanian soldier,
fighting under our command, with his bare hands.
Some old grievance from Danov's village. Only
Danov's record saved him. He wiped out a German
machine gun nest with rifle bullets, grenades, then
his clubbed rifle. Killed eight men. No matter. Talk to
them."

"What do I say?"

"Ask one of them to tell the story of the Molotov

cocktail. They all know it and maybe you can get someone to stand up."

Bronya takes me home that evening. She smiles more now, has forgotten her limp. She proudly shows me six knives, spoons, and forks that she and her friends have bought for company dinners. "We will take turns," she says. "Two of us have men friends. You're my friend, Max," and she pokes me in the chest. "There is room enough for all four girls and four friends if we share the silverware and some bring their own. Soon we will give a big party. What's the matter, Max? Why so quiet tonight?"

I hug her to me on the narrow bed.

"You're hurting me, Max. What is that?" And she reaches under my shirt and puts her hand on the haft of my knife. "Why a knife, Max? Talk, dearest Max. Please talk."

I tell her about the Cossack. She hugs me, kisses me, strains me to her thin body. I look over her shoulder at the new spoons and forks.

When I get back to the barracks, I take out my whetstone, go downstairs to the back of the building, and in the darkness, I take out my spoon and start to file the end with my stone. I fashion a crude point. I practice holding the spoon end and jabbing the air with the sharpened handle. Then I try to slip it into my boot. No good. I can't walk without cutting myself. I dash the spoon against the wall. Then I bend down and pick it up, break off the point; and now I have a baby spoon. No help here.

I can't sleep, awaken tired out.

All I can think about while I'm at the sewing machine is the coming lesson.

The men file in, sit on the two benches against the wall.

I stand before them, naked. "Comrades, yesterday you heard an interesting story from Comrade Teodorov about the fierce fighters of the Soviet Army, the Red Cossacks." I pause, look at each of them, like I have never looked before: ordinary men, from the young Cossack on the far left to the bearlike Danov to the right. "Can any of you tell us the story of the discovery of the Molotov cocktail?"

Silence.

"In your own words, comrades, any one."

The third man from the left stands up. He tugs on his overshirt, clears his throat.

"Begin, comrade," I say encouragingly. "We are listening."

"There was this tank man. I'll call him Nicolai although I don't remember his name. The German tanks were attacking the city . . . Leningrad or Moscow . . . or some such city . . . I am a country man myself, comrades, a peasant and to me all cities are alike.

"The brave lads in this city had built tank road blocks in the streets to stop the Germans. They tore up buildings, built earth mounds with iron posts sticking from them, took huge rocks from the river, I don't know what river, comrades, and added these rocks to the road block. They they built a second and a third road block across the main road in case the Germans could get over the first two. Our lads worked twelve, fourteen hours without stopping.

One young girl, it is told, filled her apron with dirt because her hands were bleeding from holding the shovel in the cold. And she piled the dirt apronful after apronful on top of the third barrier, between the rocks.

"The German tanks smashed through and over the first and second road blocks. Lots of tanks now, firing as they came, tanks as thick as horseflies around a pile of horseshit. A single Russian tank came up from the other way to meet them. I'm sorry, comrades, I can't remember the name of the tank but it was one of our big ones. A few infantrymen hanging onto the tank."

Levitsky appears at the open doorway and stands there, listening.

"Now one tank man, a simple peasant like myself, had too much to drink the night before. The tank stalled on our side of the road block. Our guns kept firing. This peasant tank man had two empty vodka bottles at his feet and another one half full."

Levitsky disappears from the doorway.

"Our tank ran out of ammunition. The soldiers scrambled out and began firing their rifles. How to stop the oncoming German tanks, comrades? How? Our tank man, the peasant I am telling you about, comes out of the stalled tank carrying three vodka bottles. He fills them with gasoline from the stalled tank. Imagine, comrades, he poured out one half bottle of vodka. . . ." He waits expectantly for laughter, but there is not a sound. "The soldier takes wadding from his winter jacket, plugs the bottle ends, and takes matches from his pocket and . . ."

The young Cossack jumps to his feet. "I am tired,

Teacher. Enough talk today." He stretches and strolls toward the door.

In one leap, I am at the doorway, barring his way.

He stops. Such innocent blue eyes in his head.

I reach inside my waistband. No knife, so I scratch my belly, a terrible itch.

"What are you looking for," the Cossack says, "a pencil?"

I can't speak. I'm a dead hero.

He takes a step closer. Ten feet separate us.

A growl from the last man on the right hand bench. He stands, a black beard like Abraham, hand clenched like a hammer. "Danov speaks from the Lithuanian Division." The Cossack turns half way round. "I fought with the twelve thousand from the Sixteenth Division. Two thousand Jews died in the snow at Alekseyevka. Our cry when we charged the Nazi machine guns—*far unsere tattes un mammes*—for our fathers and mothers.

"I gave this arm for the motherland," and he wags his left stump, "and I would give the other one. Sit down!" he thunders.

The Cossack flushes a deep pink. "I only wanted a cigarette."

"Why didn't you say so, Yermak? Please sit down and I'll give you a smoke." I reach into my pocket, take out some *makhorka*, sit on the floor and with a page from *Pravda*, begin making cigarettes. I make four, get up and pass them out. "I have no matches, Yermak," I say to him, passing him the first cigarette. Four cigarettes for eight men.

"Share, comrades," and I turn my back on them and look out the only window. A truck rolls into the yard and two workers begin to unload hides. I hear the striking of a match. When I turn back, four men are smoking and the cigarettes pass from hand to hand. The room fills with smoke.

That afternoon, like in my other life as a barber, my hands work by themselves. Upper after upper piles up next to me. Levitsky comes over twice, inspects one or two uppers and puts them back on my finished pile.

Here comes Teodorov. I watch him as he threads his way between the sewing machines. He looks down at me. "Now Max . . . are you finally . . . really going to help the Soviet?" He wears a little smile that I've never seen before. I misjudged him. And that's dangerous. The man is not a fool. A fanatic yes, but not a fool. I know he has heard everything. There must be an informer among the eight who reports to him.

"Teodorov—why even in this warm weather, the summer time, you still wear your quilted jacket?"

"It's the snow and the cold, Max. For me, there is always snow. I can never get warm."

No school and no Teodorov for a few days and now my head is never still. I tell Bronya that I will teach my class how to write their names, how to read. I will become a real teacher. I must get pencils and writing paper. I'll keep this to myself until I get a chance to speak to Teodorov alone. Where is he? When will he come back?

I think of Bronya often while my hands work. I have not taken her to bed . . . not yet . . . what will it be like? Like the others . . . no . . . not like with the she-bear.

And then she will only be my fifth woman.

At the end of the last work day, Danov, pushing his broom with his right hand, passes in front of my sewing machine. He pauses and runs the broom back and forth before my eyes.

"Danov, I have been looking for you . . . to thank you for your help with the Cossack."

He leans on the broom. "Next time, you will handle him yourself. That kind always comes back." He stands there as if he wants to say more. "He could break you in two, Teacher. Carry your knife with you and kill him when he starts in again. Hold the knife tightly," he tightens his grip on the broom. "Place your other hand over and around the knife hand on the haft." He looks at his stump. "Step close to him— don't strike from a distance, both hands around the haft, so he can't wrestle the knife from your hand. Jab upwards to the belly." Danov steps close to me as I get up from my chair. He jabs the broom into my belly, just touching my belt. "Like a bayonet, keep jabbing, kill him, Teacher." He turns and walks off, pushing the broom before him, stump wagging, not tightly held at his side as usual.

They've made him crazy too, that Danov. One Danov is equal to a squad of eight men at the front; but in prison, he'd not last a week.

On Sunday, no work, and Bronya tells me of a forest outside the city. A few blocks on the hard-packed sand streets, then we turn into Lenin Street, cross the crushed stone gutter, onto the concrete sidewalk and continue to the square and bandstand where the band is tuning up for the afternoon's dancing. After a while, we turn down another sandy street which soon turns into a country road.

We pass fields of green-striped watermelon. A clanking tractor belching gray smoke forces us off the road. Then farther on, a log house with straw-thatched roof and smoke rising from the chimney; beside the house, a small garden with green feathery tops of carrots. I never noticed colors before. Dig potatoes, steal, run, eat them. Hide. Steal carrots too. And cabbages. Anything. I never thought how these foods came from the earth.

She turns down a path and I follow. Still and dark among the fir trees until we come to a pond flooded by golden sunlight. A frog leaps from the bank into the water. Splash. A fish rises and with a twist of its body, disappears.

Ducks, wings flapping, rise from the pond. "Look at them, how beautiful," she says, with a tug on my sleeve.

I try to count the ducks. They change partners: four, three, and two fly in formation; then three, four, and four. I count eleven when suddenly, the flock wheels and skims over the treetops. Another turn, the flock breaks apart and reforms into four, yet another four, and another. Twelve ducks, I am sure, fly over the alders and white birches.

The summer will soon be over. Already the air is sharpening when I leave the factory at night to walk to the cafeteria and Bronya.

When I turn the corner onto Lenin Street, I see Teodorov far off, his quick walk, on the other side of the street. In my haste to catch him alone, tell him my idea, I trip on a raised sidewalk slab. I spring up, an ankle pain, ignore it, and hurry to cross the street. A black car cuts in front of me and pulls up to the sidewalk. I turn, walk back to the nearest building wall, sit down on the concrete and pretend to roll a cigarette.

Teodorov walks, a man follows. The man trots to keep up. The car driver steps out and walks toward Teodorov. Stops in front of him. The runner catches up with Teodorov, grabs his arm and from under his coat, he takes out a pistol. Jams the barrel into Teodorov's side. I can guess what they are saying. Like the time in Lublin, the sound failed in the movie house. The American gangsters in broad-brimmed hats were waiting outside a saloon. I knew what would happen when the swinging door flew open.

And now . . .

Teodorov waves his good hand in the air. What a talker, he was. The driver listens patiently. Then with Teodorov between them, they walk back to the car. In goes the driver, then Teodorov in the back seat, followed by the NKVD gunman. The car starts slowly.

I raise my hand to greet Teodorov, then start scratching my head. Fool! The driver is looking out the car window. Teodorov sits stony-faced. Did he see me wave?

Good-bye, Teodorov the Bulgarian.

Good-bye.

The next day the eight students in my class have disappeared. I will not ask Levitsky. Or anyone. After lunch, I see the peasant-tankman who told the Molotov cocktail story working at his machine. I thought it would be—not the Cossack or Danov or the tankman—but one of the other five. I guessed wrong.

The classroom filled with ugly brown women's shoes. Thousands of shoes. No one came to take them away. After a while, one could barely close the door.

I wait for them to pick me up. I can't run again. I wait.

SEVEN

When I knock on the door, I hear Inger's "Come in."

Inger looks at me, a hard look, then turns to the other two women. "We were just leaving. Come on girls, put on your coats, we'll take a walk."

A groan from a chunky young girl. "Come!" Inger says, throwing a coat at the heavy one. She shoos the two women out the door, turns to look at me, shakes her head, then slams the door.

I don't take off my coat, walk toward Bronya, arms outstretched. "How old are you? The truth."

Three feet separate us. "Almost sixteen."

"Sixteen! My God! Sixteen."

She grabs me by the throat. Scratches my neck, tears at my beard. Nothing to me, I've been beaten by experts, by she-bears, Uzbeks. I grab her thin wrists.

"Sixteen, sixteen," she says. "It's old enough. Where have you been? Where do you eat?" She slaps my left cheek. It stings. She runs back to her bed, sits, buries her head in her hands, shoulders shaking. Cries. Her crying stops.

I move toward her, sit down and start to embrace her. She shifts away. I hear a muffled, "Go, Max, go. The longer you stay, the harder it is."

I get up, stroke her hair, turn and walk to the door. I hesitate, "I'll be back Bronya, I swear to you."

She raises her head, "If only I could believe you."

So I go back to her and take her to bed. While I am inside the warm good place and she knows little but tries to love me, I am alone. Thinking, and thinking is no good. Her thin matchstick legs wrap around me in a tight embrace, yet I think on and then with relief, fly off. Her legs untangle. "Can I believe you now, Max?" she says. Then as I hug her to me, kiss her over and over, her last words, "I must believe."

For several days, I see the same man lurking outside the factory when I finish work.

I start wearing my knife in a sheath that I've made from scrap leather. I wonder if he's a four-letter man.

A light snowfall that evening. Everyone has left. Just the hammering of one of the cobblers who is resoling my fine leather boots. I am lucky to be wearing my felt-lined *valenki* tonight.

I sit in front of my machine. Bronya ignores me when I come to her work place at night; food scarce now in the cafeteria. They even ran out of bread and for the past few nights served only sunflower seeds, a watery soup, and watermelon. I chew on a piece of licorice, sickly sweet, but it stops my hunger pains. The walls and concrete floor are cold and while I was sewing earlier, I stopped to warm my fingers under my armpits.

The cobbler's footsteps echo in the empty room and he hands me my boots and I give him fifty roubles. "Good night, Alexis," I call to his retreating back. Levitsky has not spoken to me or examined my work since Teodorov was taken. Then I smell the sour odor of sheep fat and hear the broom scraping along. The swarthy Kalmyk turns into my aisle and sweeps under my machine. He wants to sell a foxskin cap like the one he is wearing. We haggle and finally, he agrees to twenty-five roubles. Just what I need for winter. I put on the cap and remember a Kazakh proverb: from a pack of dogs, even a fox will not escape.

On with my sheepskin, and I take my resoled boots in one hand and go to the street side of the factory. Push a stool near the wall and step up to peer through the high window. He's there, rubbing his hands together to keep warm. Waiting. Can't be the police; they'd just pull out a pistol and grab me. I close my hand around my knife haft, open my middle coat button so I can pull the knife quickly, and boots in the other hand, I walk out. I'm ready for him.

I avoid the dark places near the buildings and walk in the gutter. My feet slide over new ice in the ditches or where it is thinner, crunch the ice cracks and I step into ankle-deep water.

"Don't turn, Max," I hear. "Keep walking!"

I wheel around, face the voice, knife out. Drop the boots. "Why have you been following me?" I ask him. "Talk!"

He stands ten feet away, on the balls of his feet, like a fighter. "It's me, Dov." Raising his earflaps, he takes off his cap. "Don't you recognize me?"

That face. It can't be. The other man was a powerful giant. He has shrunken, my King of Thieves. I draw myself up to my full height, knife still ready.

"Put that knife away, Max." He grins, lips pull back, no teeth on the right side. "You've gotten taller, Max. Do you always stand up straight now?"

"What do you want of me, thief?"

"Where can we talk? Not here in the street."

"Turn around, just walk ahead and stay in front of me." I resheath my knife and follow him. "Turn right, that's it. There's an old shed, head for it."

Door torn off the shed. I peer inside. No one. I lean against the shed wall near the open doorway. Dov moves alongside.

"Your sister wants to see you," he says. "A fine boy, she has; he's two years old."

"You have a message from her? Did she send you? How's my father?"

"He's older, alive."

"That's some bridegroom you found for my sister Genia. A real prize."

"Her little boy looks and walks like you, Max. She's baking another."

"You came six hundred miles to tell me Genia is pregnant?"

"No. The Ukrainian dog is back from the front. He's starting up again."

"So?"

"Let's go inside the hut, Max. It's warmer. You're practically a Siberian. We southerners are not used to this cold."

"Why go inside? Have your say. Are you through? I'm hungry."

"Max, come in with me." He reaches into his pocket and takes out two meat pasties. "Take one, eat. Then a sip or two of vodka," and he pats his pocket.

"You go first."

Inside, it is at least out of the wind and I accept a meat pasty and a long swallow of vodka.

He passes me the bottle again. "We have to stop him, that Ukrainian, and we need you."

"You're crazy or you must think I'm crazy. One more brush with the police and I'm in jail for life. Or worse. Not a warm one in Alma Ata either. In Siberia! Remember that Jewish judge in Ili. He fixed him good."

"Not good enough. He sent him to the front lines and the Ukrainian lost an arm. Better if he lost two arms and two legs."

"Don't tell me any more!"

"He and his other hero veterans are beating on us. Won't let us sell; we're afraid to go to the bazaars."

"Why us? Why is it always the Jews, the Jews?"

"On a bent twig, jump all the goats." Three men walk by, huddled together, heads down against the snow that is now falling thick and fast. They start for the shed, but when I appear in the doorway, they turn away.

Dov takes another swallow, shakes the vodka bottle and sails it through the open doorway. "Max, Max," he goes on, "they break our bones."

"Give them back."

"Max, they burned Pavel's beard. Set him afire. Broke both his legs."

"I'm going now, don't follow me."

"I'll meet you tomorrow. Think it over."

The next day, he is bolder and follows me openly as I turn down the same side street; the snow crunching underfoot, air crisp and sharp after the stuffy factory. He turns with me and draws alongside. "We need you, Max."

"Again, need me! Get the porters. A few tough Jews among them. How about your own pick-pockets?"

"I asked. Many times. They won't do it."

"Why us? Always us. The Germans gas us, burn us. The Russians starve us, freeze us. The Ukrainians break our bones. Why? Why?"

"You know why, Max. We're the Chosen People." We walk in silence past the shed, now smoke is coming from a hole in the roof.

"Dov, I have a girl. It's quiet here. A regular job. I don't want to wander, to run off again. Some day, I'll go back home. Get married. Take up my old trade. Open my own shop."

"You're still a barber? With that untrimmed beard?

There are all kinds of tales about you in the South. You wrestled a bear, killed it with a knife. You've become . . . I don't know how to say it."

"Say it."

"The Messiah can return as a barber. Why not?"

"Ah, Dov, I see. Now you write your own Scripture. Make up Bible stories for children."

"Don't make fun, Max. Don't joke with me. I didn't want to come this far to try and get you. There is no one else. If you come, if I tell them you are coming, I can get others. Your father still trades a little. Do you want him beaten up? Killed?"

"I'll come, Dov, but I don't want to kill anyone."

"We'll take care of that."

"No killing. A good beating is enough. I'll come, Dov."

He embraces me and I hug him to me. He pounds my back, breathes vodka-garlic into my face. I'm caught.

"I knew you would help. Here is your ticket to Alma Ata. To throw them off your scent. But you are to get off at Ili. Someone will meet you. Take these roubles. Here," and he stuffs money in my overcoat pocket. "Stay quiet, inside where our guide will take you until we are ready."

"When shall I leave?"

"Tomorrow. Do they check the sleeping quarters?"

"No. We're contract workers. No need. And I may have a day's head start. I don't think my foreman will say anything the first day I'm absent."

"Good. Once I tell a friend of yours that you're coming, he will help us. He used to be a boxer, not too smart, but very strong."

It must be Berchik from the logging camp. "He's not dumb, tries to appear dumb, that friend."

"One thing more: your father is now in Ili. Genia has taken him in. Don't try to see them, Max. The fewer who know you are there, the safer for all of us."

On the way back to the barracks, I fall into Kazakh thinking, that old riddle: I fell into an abyss without noticing it. Where do I get out?

EIGHT

In the barracks, I take off my coat, throw it on the bed and examine my possessions. I am a man of property: two blankets, two extra shirts, underwear, a foxtail cap, an Uzbek *tyubeteika*, and an Uzbek torn quilted robe. Leave it all behind, like a good party man. I have the roubles I've saved pinned inside my shirt, always carry them with me; have Dov's roubles in the jacket pocket. I take out my knife, resharpen the point, wonder if it can go easily through a heavy sheepskin, and touch up the blade. I slice a few black hairs from my beard, then cut off some hair from my arm, still blond here like my head when I was a child. No one bothers to look up at me. Men doze. Play cards, smoke. These beds nearby change bodies. I've made no friends here. If only I had something to leave for Bronya, some gift. Maybe she can use the underwear. I take out a pencil and start to write.

Dearest Bronya,

I know you are angry with me and right to be angry. You are old enough. For anything. I love you very much. I cannot live without you.

When the war is over, I will ask you to marry me.

Please, darling Bronya, when the war is over and it is safe to travel, meet me in front of the Town Hall in Zamoscz. Or ask about me there. I will not leave Zamoscz until you come. DO NOT SPEAK OR ASK ABOUT ME WHEN I AM GONE.

I must go away for a while.

I wanted to say these things before, tell you of my love but . . . it never seemed the right time. Believe me!

So good-bye, my beloved Bronya, until we meet once more and then we will never be parted.

Max

I stuff the Uzbek cap in my pocket, put on the foxskin cap and coat, and head for Bronya's house.

Cold. The snow has stopped and I leave fresh footprints so I decide to take a roundabout route. A bright three-quarter moon lights my path. Slip my note under her door and steal away.

In the morning, I get up at the hour when I usually leave for the factory. I munch a piece of stale bread and chew on a withered apple. Always I've kept emergency food.

On my way to the railroad, I switch caps, put on my Uzbek *tyubeteika* and drop the foxtail into a hole, kick snow over it. I carry my metal cup, still have a handful of prunes for the train ride, touch the knife haft in its sheath, check the roubles pinned into my shirt pocket, check the roubles in my coat—never traveled in such style before, a man with money and his own ticket.

I try to doze in the crowded compartment. I turn up my sheepskin collar, want no talk with the fat woman, her bundles next to me, or the Russians across the aisle, nor with the official-looking man in a long fur coat, carrying a briefcase.

To sleep, eyes closed, rest . . . my father's face swims before me . . . he keeps shaking his head sadly . . . trying to say something . . . his mouth opens and closes like a carp out of water . . . no words come out . . . he looks young and strong . . . how I respected him . . . longed for his good opinion.

Then I am back on Kazakh land. Kazakh means outlaw, I have been told, and these nomads do not bend easily to the rulers. A violent people, the Kazakhs . . . my friend Janim Batir would be better suited for this job than me . . . Janim ready to hunt and kill the Koreans . . . sure they had eaten his dog . . . his father said the skilled man is often without a knife . . . I want to take out my blade,

check for sharpness, not here . . . later . . . must
sleep . . . get rid of these thoughts . . . think of
women, women. . . .

The girl who loved the bathhouse told me when we
first met, she loved a man, slept with him in the
cotton fields, but her father called her beloved a
muzhik, and this Bukhara Jew betrothed her to
another. I wept, she said, a river flowed, but my
father insisted I marry his bridegroom. So I ran away
and came to you. Max, you did not mind that I'd slept
with another.

I should mind! She was only my second woman
. . . funny looking and pockmarked but how she
loved to fuck. To fuck and go to the bathhouse, as if
the bathhouse were her *mikvah*, that would cleanse
her of lovemaking. I tired of her face and her talk
always about the man she really loved. Once, I am on
top of her and she cries out his name!

Anna strikes me again and again . . . I want to
smash her this time . . . blacken her eyes . . . I
throw her down . . . pull down her drawers . . .
turn her over and spank her large white bottom. She
cries, sorry now that she ever struck me . . . too
late . . . Anna-Ursula, you're not a real woman
anyway . . . she gets on hands and knees, head
down, bare behind winking an invitation . . . just a
big, smooth satiny bear . . . who wants a bear
. . . sharp yellow teeth . . . sharp claws. I have a
real girl now . . . thin, and she loves me, only me,
like a girl should.

I'm in a panic, can't breathe . . . can't remember
her name . . . what is it . . . open my eyes . . .
close them . . . look out the window . . . sandy

earth . . . scrubby trees . . . a fine woman . . .
she respects me . . . a woman for children . . . a
home . . . her name, her name, her name is *Bronya*.

When we reach Ili, I get off quickly, mingle with the
crowd, only thirty or so; the other passengers will go
on to Alma Ata or down the line, west to Chymkent
or Tashkent.

Someone will meet you, Dov the thief had said. I'd
asked what he would look like. You don't have to
know, he replied. He will say to you, do you
remember the drunken rabbi, and he will be your
guide.

Like a pickpocket, an Uzbek boy appears at my
side. He gives the password in broken Russian, and I
follow closely behind him.

Past the bathhouse, through a winding maze of
streets, one clay house after another; round and
round he goes, my young guide. Does he think he is
confusing me? Perhaps, but I know Ili from my
bathhouse days.

Finally, my guide darts into a small hut, just one
room, and I wonder if he sleeps here alone. As if he
read my mind, he says, "There are two other couples
here, gone away now, to Chymkent to trade." The
boy takes out bread and soft cheese and vodka, two
glasses and he motions me to sit down. He lays out
the food on a bench and we sit cross-legged on either
side. An old-young man, not bar mitzvah age yet I'm
sure. We eat quickly. The boy hands me the bottle
with a princely gesture. I take a swig, hand it back
and he takes a swallow. He looks directly at me as if

he is taking my measure. Too young for this business ahead but I like him.

Then he takes out a blue velvet bag trimmed with a Star of David, opens the sack and takes out *tefellin*.

With his right hand, he winds the phylacteries around his left arm, his forehead, then begins to sway and chant.

Yithgadal veyithka dash sheme raba
bealma diverra hiroute
veamlih malhoute
Veyatsman pourkane

And on he goes, shaking and swaying, while his loose pants flap with his prayers.

I smile to myself. Two things I am good at: barbering and languages. Stealing food too. I can always pick up a new tongue. I'll become a teacher in my next life, teach Polish—who wants it? Russian—bad memories. Jewish—learn it at your mother's knee or don't bother. I'll emigrate to Palestine with Bronya and learn Hebrew, become a farmer. Or America and learn English, open my own barber shop, live among Jews, hire six men, get rich, take care of my father and sister, have many children, never go hungry, feed any stranger who arrives at our home . . . Bronya's and mine.

Ose shalom
bimromax
ou berahamav
yaase shalom a lenou veal
Yisrael veimrou amen.

Kaddish! That kid recited the Prayer for the Dead. For me! I look at him closely. Who is he? A dybbuk, a prophet dressed in rags; they dressed in rags in the olden days.

The boy carefully unwinds his phylacteries and puts them back in his hiding place. A red mark around his forehead where the leather cut into his skin. Eyes shining, he looks up, "If only I had my father's rifle, we'd finish them off." He sits down on the bench. I lean back against the wall. "How will you kill the Ukrainian?" he says. "With your knife?"

"Shut up! They promised me a silent guide, not a big-mouthed kid!"

The boy pulls back as if struck; eyes narrow; he swallows and his Adam's apple pops.

No need for an enemy. I must win him back. I switch to Yiddish, "Tell me about your father's rifle."

"You want to hear?" His voice comes from far off, takes on the sing-song of a story teller. "Our people are from Derbent, a Dagestani port on a pass between the mountains and the Caspian Sea. In the valley of the Jews. We fought the Russians with sword and rifle hundreds of years ago. My grandfather told me many stories."

"I never heard of your people."

"Few have. We are called Mountain Jews, and came from Persia, driven by Moslen persecutions to Dagestan in the northeastern Caucasus."

"You are a learned young man, know Hebrew and are steeped in Torah, not like myself. I know little."

"You fought the giant brown bear. That is enough. Also we heard how you beat off six Uzbeks with your staff. If I had a few more Tat countrymen, we'd handle these Ukrainians our own way. My father is dead. They killed him." He gets up from the bench and sits on his blanket against the wall.

"How old are you?"

"Fourteen."

Is he lying? He's had a harder life than me. My bad times started later, almost eighteen when we fled from Zamoscz. The children here all look younger than their real age. Little food, dressed in rags. And when they become young men, they age quickly, like myself—I look forty. The boy does not want to talk now. He sits there and stares into space.

The orange light disappears and it turns eggplant purple, then coffee black. Night arrives. The boy rummages under another blanket, pulls out a long knife in a sheath. He slides it half way out, feels the blade, slips it back. Gets up and starts to tie the knife around his waist.

I spring to my feet. "Put the knife away."

He looks up in surprise. "I always wear it."

"Not now. A young man with a knife is easily remembered."

"I am naked without it."

"Put it away! In a minute, you'll start telling me about your honor as a Jew. Now listen carefully, my young guide. We want to do the job, not get caught. And live. Live! Do you understand? You are my guide. That's all."

He stands frozen, like a snapshot.

I wait, can't take the knife from him by force.

He puts his hand on the knife haft. Son of a bitch. The kid is crazy.

"With that knife, you are of no use to me, to our cause. I'll find another guide," and I turn my back on him, go to the doorway and open the door. I half turn around and see the boy toss the knife in the corner.

"You are my guide. Come. I need your help."

The boy says thoughtfully, "Please wait here for me. This may not be the night. I must speak to the king."

I search for the right words.

He stands before me, brown head at chin level. "Please let me pass. I can't tell you my name. I know your name."

I grasp his shoulders, tighten my grip, then step aside. The door shuts. I sink onto his blanket. His knife presses into my back so I reach under and push it out of the way.

I doze off, awaken when I hear the door open. The boy enters, crouches down beside me. "He did not come tonight. The king says to tell you, you are to come with me tomorrow and the next day and the next if necessary. It is your job to stop the Ukrainian, hold him up for a few seconds. The others will do the rest. Now go to sleep; you must be tired."

The boy gets under the blanket next to me. He keeps his distance. I'm spoiled, soft from sleeping in a bed too long; can't get to sleep and soon I hear his even breathing. Some time that night, I get chilled, have kicked off the blanket. Like he has not slept, the boy appears on his knees and draws the blanket up to my chin, gets back in and tucks it around our bodies. His shoulder touches my back.

My brother, my son.

The first night, the one-armed Ukrainian walks with two men on either side. The one-legged man with a crutch throws his head back and laughs a wild laugh. The man with the cane takes out a bottle and it passes from hand to hand as each man takes a drink. Just ordinary men, neither tall nor short. I lie curled up at the junction of a house and an alley, resting against the wall, eyes half-closed. They take no notice of me.

During the day, I doze or pace the hut. Four paces one way; five paces the other way. The boy brings food and we eat together. He refuses to take my roubles. I piss into an old pot. The boy empties it. When it grows dark, I go outside to relieve myself. I know the street now; it's called Alley of the Jews.

Another night and this time, they are drunk, the three of them, reeling, holding on to one another. "Good," the boy says, "now they are drunk like always. The king wants him alone."

I change my station so after a few days, I am farther down the street.

I have rehearsed my playacting so many times while waiting for the Ukrainian that my mind begins to wander tonight. My sister Genia's face appears: how she washed her brown, round arms while I carried water for her bath; her house only a few streets away—she could pass by now, never recognize me. Bronya walks in bare feet over a richly carpeted floor. After we eat, reclining on cushions, with plates of food between us, drinking cup after cup of scalding tea, I undress her and start to kiss her, from her little feet, to her legs, up to the inside of her thighs, over them to her secret place, her navel, gently I kiss her, her little breasts, then glue my mouth to hers. I *must* not lose her. Too many have gone away . . . lost . . . there can be no other.

The night grows chillier.

They come again, drunk, not staggering, but happily drunk and singing a Cossack song I've heard before.

All their thoughts they thought as one.
And as the summer passed, the warmth of summer,
And winter came, brothers, the chilly winter,
How and where, brothers, shall we spend the winter?
To move on to the Yaik is a long, long march.

The voices are fading . . .

And if we wander along the Volga, all will think us
thieves;
If on to Kazan city, we go, there is the Czar;
Like the menacing Czar, Ivan Vasilievich . . .

Shouts. Laughter. The man with the crutch stands on one leg and fences the veteran with the cane. How can such savages sing like a choir of angels?

The boy tells me later: we cannot wait much longer. Tomorrow night, one, two, or three men, if they are drunk enough—we strike!

An overcast night, thick clouds hide the sliver of a moon. A swift fierce rain shower and I am soaked, lie against the clay wall, shivering. The boy runs to my side, sits down and whispers. "Ready, Max. He comes alone." The first time he's used my name.

I get to my feet, dry my hands against my pants legs; then drape the coat over and around my right arm, knife hidden under my coat. My left arm swings free. The Ukrainian turns the corner and marching along, he moves steadily toward me.

I take a few steps into his path, then fall to my knees, knife ready. I pray he is soused with vodka. "Help an old comrade. A drink, a few roubles. Help me."

The Ukrainian seems as sober as a commissar. He veers off at an angle as if trying to avoid passing me. I cry louder, "Have pity, comrade, they took an arm from me, can't you even spare a few kopecks?"

He spins on his heel, changing direction and warily comes toward me. I remember the chicken I killed, how she bled.

Fifty feet away, forty. Where are they? When will they come? I'll throw off the coat. One thrust to his belly and twist the knife.

He stops, grasps his nose with two fingers, blasts, and wipes the snot on his pants.

A rush of feet. I watch the Ukrainian advance; his knife appears, makes little darting circles before him. The king smashes a club against the Ukrainian's head. He falls to his knees without a sound, pitches forward. Another club blow from a second man. It's Berchik, the forest giant.

They make him dead.

Now they are kicking him, Berchik and another: heavy-booted kicks from either side. His head wags back and forth—how does it stay attached to the neck? The King of Thieves watches, leaning on his club.

Where is the boy, my guide?

I wonder when the Ukrainian died.

The two men drag the body away, each man holding a leg, into an alley. "Get up, off your knees," the king says to me. "It's finished. Go!"

NINE

Go where? I sit on the hard ground. The others disappear, not a soul, not a sound in the street. If a donkey could fly, I'd steal one and with Bronya sitting in front of me, I'd take off for faraway Samarkand, the magic city, on the old Chinese silk route. But with my luck, when I arrived, I'd find a typhus epidemic and thousands of starving Jewish refugees.

I must see my sister once more, then find the boy. I get up, replace the knife in its sheath and walking at a fast pace, turn a few corners and quickly arrive at my sister's *kibitka*. A dogs howls down the street. How did he escape being eaten? Too late to turn back and no place to hide. I stand there, I don't know for how long, staring at her doorway.

The door opens and the husband walks out. He walks shakily; his feet get tangled; he drops his cigarette, reaches down for it; the wind rises and blows it away. He tried to retrieve it and falls to his knees. As he stretches for it, it's blown out of reach. He crawls after it, traps it under his cupped hand and puts the cigarette between his lips. Draws on it. It's gone out.

With a few steps, I come to him, stand over him.

He stares at my shoes, up to my knees, my face. "You're out? They let you out?"

I shove his shoulder. He falls over and rolls on the ground. It would be so easy to get rid of this trash but. . . .

He pushes himself up, sits there. "Your sister is with child. That should make you happy. Come in, have a drink. Let's celebrate together like real family."

Over the housetops, the sky glows. It spreads—a rosy colored light. The dog barks again, then yelps in fear. They've butchered him.

I turn away and run toward the Street of the Jews. Dark figures in army castoffs are running around the huts. Billows of smoke from the windows and doors of the first three huts. One man dips torches in a barrel of gasoline; others grab the torches, light them and fling them through the windows of the huts. Doors are battered down. The veterans run in, clubs in hand, and drag people into the street. Others follow and fire the huts. Knife in hand, I move ahead, keeping close to the building walls. A muzhik emerges from a hut on my left, dragging an old man by the collar. He drops his hold, raises his club over his head. I step close to him, catch a glancing blow on my upraised arm, and slip the knife into his belly. Pull it out and run ahead. Hoarse shouting, "Kill the Jews! Traitors! Kill them. Don't let one Jew escape."

Our refuge is in flames. No way I can get through the door and find the boy. A peasant comes up to me, waving his club. "No one is there," I say, waving my bloody knife, "go to the other huts. Don't let one of them escape."

I slow down, my bloody knife my passport. A rock strikes my back. I turn and a boy reaches into a sack for another rock. I menace him with the knife and he runs off.

I dart between our hut and the next one and at the back of the row of huts, I peer out. Men are stationed like outposts cutting off my escape route in this direction. In the open field to my right, an officer sits on horseback, waving his saber. He dispatches men with clubs to the right and left. This is not ordinary pogrom I realize. The leader is using the pogromists like a cavalry regiment: hold the middle and turn the flanks.

I'll be worse off in the open where the men with clubs can run me down. I drift back to the street, knife in hand. A muzhik runs by, club in one hand, samovar in the other. A woman moans on the ground, her skirt flung over her head, a man astride her; others wait their turn. I'm helpless.

More looters run by carrying coats, pots; one with an armful of dresses.

A squad of six men march up the street, staves like rifles over their shoulder. A crowd follows, knives, sickles or iron bars in their hands. I wave my knife in the air, shout, "Kill the Jews," with the mob and fall in with the stragglers, hurrying toward the last two huts.

A bearded man bursts our of a doorway, carrying a stool in front of him. He smashes the stool over an attacker's head, then tries to cut between two burning huts; a club strikes him across the knees, more blows and he is surrounded by booted men, kicking at him. A giant one-armed veteran leaps on his back with both heels. A single shriek that chills my bones, cuts to my heart, my lungs; I'm choking, the smoke, the heat, can't breathe.

Three people emerge from the last hut. A lean man in a captain's tunic, covered with medals. A boy holding a knife stands at his left; on his right, a young fellow holds a wooden bench. Two women follow, each with a knife in hand.

The captain steps forward, raises his right hand. "Comrades! I am Captain Kagan. I fought under General Chernyakhovsky against the Nazi invaders." A rock flies into the air and the young fellow guarding the officer fends it off with his bench. "What are you doing, acting like hooligans—men who lived and fought with honor—veterans of our glorious struggle for the motherland," a few more rocks, but no one is hit, "tell your leader, comrade-soldiers, that Captain Kagan wants to speak to him."

If only I could have the courage to stand beside that captain, at his side, defend him and the woman with my body.

The attackers mill around, leaderless. The one-armed giant urges them on. He waves his iron bar. They won't move. He steps up to the captain and swings the bar over his head; the captain steps back; the bar strikes the ground at his feet. The captain rests his hand on the giant's shoulder, says something I can't hear; then he coughs, a fit of coughing strikes him and he spits at his feet. The giant drops the bar and retreats into the crowd.

Now the rocks begin to fly. First, a few high in the air and the young man bats them away with his bench. Then more rocks. One strikes the captain's elbow. Another hits the boy in the temple. He falls and the younger woman drags him back into the house.

The captain grabs the knife from the gray haired woman. He holds it before him like a bayonet. "Anti-revolutionary scum. Cowardly dogs! Come on. I'll unbutton your bellies."

Now he's done it. A brave fool, I'm looking at a dead man, but he doesn't know it.

He's fuming away, puffed up like a rooster. Thrusts the air with his long knife. "I fought you White Guards in 1919—I know you Kulaks—swine—who is the first to die—come ahead—try me."

Die, fool. What do I care.

Three cars drive into the head of the street. Two swing around and block the exit. Seven, no eight men get out, pistols in hand and forming a skirmish line, walk into the mob. They halt in a ragged line and fire a volley into the air.

Time for the barber to go. A bullet from one side is the same as a broken head from the other. I slip between the huts into the field, not worried about the pickets now and I start across the field. When I look back, clouds of smoke fill the sky, flames still lick out of windows. A goat neighs, runs up to me; I push it away.

A shadow rises from the earth. My knife is ready. "Max, it's me, David, your guide. I've found you."

I hug him to me. "David. Now I know your name. Stay with me. We walk slowly; watch. No running unless I tell you. Understand?"

No one is blocking our path; a few stray sheep are grazing and I take a long detour around the far end of the field and head for my sister's house.

When I get there, the door is ajar. I go in. No on. Signs of a hurried flight. Table knocked over. Clothes lying on the floor below the hooks. Drawers in the chest are wide open. I go to the door and see two more families leaving their huts, carrying bundles and hurrying toward the railroad station.

"They are gone, David," I tell the Tat boy who stands silently at my side. "You are my family."

So our long journey began.

I bought two donkeys and we joined the refugees on the move going west. Avoided all the cities— Dzhambul, Chymkent. In Tashkent in an Uzbek *kibitka* where we stayed the night, I was bitten by a green poisonous scorpion. The boy nursed me for four days, stayed at my side with my knife in his lap. He found water and dripped it from a rag into my mouth. Somewhere, somehow, he found an orange and when I ate this orange, rind and pulp and juice, I began to recover.

Then later, he tried to trade in a small Uzbek village and not understanding the language, he made the mistake of entering an Uzbek house when the woman was home but her man was away. She started to scream and six tribesmen, knives drawn, ran toward us. Luckily I was able to speak to them and tried to explain, the young boy meant no harm—but if the headman had not arrived on his camel and pulled us upon it—we'd have died, cut to ribbons.

Many, many things happened on the way. I had to sell the donkeys just outside of Samarkand and sure enough when we got into the city, a typhus epidemic was raging.

This time—my luck held.

Neither David nor I caught the disease, although the Jews and non-Jews were dying all around us.

We lived.

TEN

I draw warmth from our Brooklyn gathering of the *landsleit* from Zamoscz. We fall on one another, hungry for the embraces of the living. We cry. This one lost both parents and a brother; another a wife and small children. There is the girl who lived near my parents' house; naked and slim she was once through a crack in the bathhouse wall: we hugged one another. She survived Buchenwald and married an American sergeant. He stands among us, an outsider, a tall stooped man in a tweed suit, dumb-

founded by our wailing. We enjoy it. Then we collect
dues for the Burial Society and then we eat—different
foods that we share among us: my wife's famous
blintzes, another's butter cookies, potato pirogen,
stuffed cabbage; drink slivovitz and vodka. And once
we laugh, when our President says, "Bye-bye Brook-
lyn." We are being evicted from this hall and must
find another place to gather.

A barber with numbers on his arm, chicken leg in
hand, calls out, "The American sergeant will help us.
Call up your President Eisenhower. Ask him can we
meet in the White House." Hungry, always hungry,
my people from Zamoscz.

I wander among the tables, searching. I avoid the
other barbers. It's a well known fact that most barbers
survived. The jailers must look neat; to look neat they
need barbers; the barbers were the last to go; some
barbers became Kapos and pushed the others into the
flames. I stay away from barbers who have had
numbers scratched into their flesh.

A neighbor offers a lift home. We leave early since
driving is bad with the streets only partly cleared
from yesterday's snowfall.

Last night, I was awakened by a stirring in the
house. Reached out for my wife. She's not there. So I
got up, no light under the bedroom doors; three
bedrooms, a nice apartment filled with my three
children and I went into the kitchen.

When I switched on the light, Bronya hid some-
thing behind her back.

"What's the matter, dearest," and I go to her with
outstretched arms.

She steps back, wipes her mouth, then raises a

blintz in a trembling hand. "Max, Max—when will I stop eating?" She turns and drops the blintz into the garbage can. Back to me, "Max—you'll stop loving me? I've gotten so fat."

"Never. Never. True, there is more of you now, just means there is more to love." I fold my arms around her. "When I met you, I had nothing. You saved me. How can I ever forget?"

I take her hand, "Come, come, let's go back to bed," and lead her to our bedroom. How stout my little Bronya has become, fatter than the circus girl who was a great strapping thing. Yes, fatter even than the conductora on the Turksib line and with just as good an appetite.

With a sigh, she gets into bed, turns away from me and curls up into a ball. I wonder what she has left untold about her wanderings, alone, from Semipalatinsk back to Zamoscz.

And I—I have told her everything, almost—a little about the she-bear and nothing about the pogromist. His coat was hanging open and my knife slipped into his belly, like cutting into a soft roll. No, I am not sorry but I have not told. Nestling against her, my hand around her waist, half-asleep, I recall the other times. Eleven years since we left the last camp in Austria, man and wife: my oldest boy now ten, a real American, talks without an accent.

I only wish that my father could see how well we live. How proud he would be if he knew I was studying at night college to become a teacher. I cut hair still but no longer feel like a barber. I study Russian, Spanish too, think in Russian sometimes, but have long lost most of the Kazakh and Uzbek language. I read Mark Twain in English and in the Russian class I read and translate Tolstoi's *Cavalry Tales*, standing before the Americans. She stirs, moans, I stroke her hip. A good wife and mother. Soon I will have enough saved so she can take her trip to Israel and visit her only living relative, a cousin. I live in Boro Park, surrounded by the Chassidim, the religious ones with their *strimmels* and long black cloaks, protected by them but not of them. I would never own a shop here. They'd make me close on Friday and Saturday. So I'm better off in my small shop in Manhattan and travel by subway every day. And back. I don't mind. My father never returned. He died in Ili, fleeing from the pogrom, in the railway station waiting room, choked with refugees. Quick. Poof, out went the candle.

Genia said he did not suffer. After a month in Moscow, she and the Hungarian and their child started back to Zamoscz. When the train crossed the border, the thief stole a Russian officer's suitcase. The train slowed down, he jumped off. So I supported Genia with her big belly and my nephew and my Bronya until the thief arrived. Three months later, he turned up in Zamoscz with money this time. First he took them to Chicago, probably found friends in the rackets there and then went on to Florida; now they are in Australia. Genia wrote that they are prospering, well and happy. Hah! If I could only believe her.

And my oldest sister, Marian, dark like a Kazakh, so strong and sure of herself—we never heard from her again. Still I dream that she may turn up, with answers for everything, like before. How could someone like her just disappear?

Ah, Bronya, I stroke her breasts, dream of Anna, the circus girl sometimes . . . forgive me.

And where is Berchik, the brave one, and the Kazakh wrestler, Konal—is he happy riding his shaggy pony and herding sheep on the windy steppes?

So many gone.

Sleep now, Max, sleep.

But he is here with me—David the Tat boy, now a handsome young man and just married to an American girl. I tried to raise him with Bronya's help but a boy like that, a hawk, raises himself. Bronya fed him well and in three years he grew taller than I am. He is now a rabbi in New Jersey, speaks like a United States Senator, and he lights my life, my brother, my son, with his love.

I get out of bed quietly and go to the window. The snow that started falling in the afternoon is still coming down. It blankets the parked cars—I must buy a little car soon—the trees and the sidewalks. Not a car drives by. The silence of a Siberian night. It's four A.M. by the clock on my dresser. What is snow to a Siberian? When Friday comes and it's time for David's visit, the streets will surely be cleared. Do you have your knife with you, Duvidl, I always ask him.

I press my forehead against the cold window pane. *Sh'ma Israel, Adonoi Elohenu, Adonoi Echod.* I find myself saying it sometimes, like now; I have not had the time yet to learn Hebrew, just know a few words. I do not believe.

Ease myself back into bed and I sniff her rich yeasty smell, like a cake baking in the oven. I lick her shoulder, taste the salt. In her sleep, she turns toward me, rests her head on my shoulder and I kiss her many times on the cheek, the forehead, her ear.

She awakens. "Max, my feet are cold."

I go to the dresser and take a pair of my warm socks from the drawer. Eyes closed, one foot at a time, she sticks out her feet. I pull on the socks.

Why sleep now when I have so much to think about? I put both hands in back of my head and stare at the ceiling. Teodorov the Bulgarian stands before me, his crippled hand in a sling, right hand waving like an orchestra leader—words in a torrent coming from his mouth. Can you still speak Teodorov, or have they stopped your mouth forever?

If I believed in the old Kazakh ways, then a man's life is divided into spans of twelve years; each span with the name of an animal—a rabbit, a fox. What am I? Not a bear. I would liked to have been a great brown bear. The ages of twenty-five and thirty-seven are especially dangerous and unlucky—next year— I'll reach the second hurdle—I may follow the Kazakh custom—give away my clothes so I can face the future in fresh clothing.

Many had it worse.

Now this bed is the only place left. I refuse to travel anywhere unless I can take the bed with me.

She turns over, away from me. I nestle close to her, clasp all of her to me with my left hand.